Praise for *The Ethical Sellout*

"Lily Zheng and Inge Hansen have written a new guidebook on the importance of managing and maintaining one's integrity as we work to navigate what they call 'the age of compromise.' I coach LGBTQ leaders and professionals on the importance of being truly authentic to oneself in all aspects of life. Zheng and Hansen wrap this all up in their book. I especially love the last line of their manifesto: 'Commit to being open to flexibility, growth, and exploration, to take up space in the world, and to live . . . life with integrity.' Authenticity is key in everything we do and become! This is a must-read!"

—David P. Whittleton, life and leadership coach and founder of Whittleton Consulting

"*The Ethical Sellout* is an honest exploration of the inevitable gray areas in which marginalized people find themselves in today's society. The book is a push-and-pull dance between the impossible pressure for absolutism shouldered by marginalized people and the need for accountability in the midst of small and big compromises. The authors take us on a journey beyond 'justification' for our choices to creating breathing room for our complex lives to be held with compassion, accountability, and possibility."

—Michelle Kim, cofounder and CEO, Awaken

"From college admissions scandals to exposés on organizations like Theranos, it is easy to point out where ethics have jumped the track. But what about our smaller, individual decisions that we make on an almost daily basis? What happens to your personal ethics when you have something to lose? This book does a masterful job of laying a framework to help you answer those questions and hear how others have struggled to come to their own conclusions."

—Todd Wilms, Chief Marketing Officer, FoundersPlace.co, and coauthor of *Beyond Product*

"Helpful, grounding, encouraging, and gentle. I needed a new way of looking at my life and my choices. This book helped me be kinder to myself at a really tough juncture—and allowed something surprising to unfold."

—Shea McGuier, Director of Communications, Telecare Corporation

"*The Ethical Sellout* combines practical advice with relatable stories—deciding how to both define and choose between your values and needs has never been more compassionately explained."
—**Stephanie Eberle, Assistant Dean and Director, Stanford BioSci Careers**

"*The Ethical Sellout* presents an uncomplicated framework for navigating the complicated choices that confront us in our increasingly complex lives as we struggle to make the compromises necessary for success without surrendering the essence of our beliefs."
—**Vineet Buch, venture capitalist and former Google executive and entrepreneur**

Sellout
The Ethical

Maintaining Your Integrity
in the Age of Compromise

Lily Zheng & Inge Hansen

BK

Berrett–Koehler Publishers, Inc.

Berrett-Koehler Publishers, Inc.
1333 Broadway, Suite 1000, Oakland, CA 94612-1921
Tel: (510) 817-2277   Fax: (510) 817-2278   www.bkconnection.com

ORDERING INFORMATION
Quantity sales. Special discounts are available on quantity purchases by corporations, associations, and others. For details, contact the "Special Sales Department" at the Berrett-Koehler address above.
Individual sales. Berrett-Koehler publications are available through most bookstores. They can also be ordered directly from Berrett-Koehler:
Tel: (800) 929-2929; Fax: (802) 864-7626; www.bkconnection.com.
Orders for college textbook / course adoption use. Please contact Berrett-Koehler: Tel: (800) 929-2929; Fax: (802) 864-7626.

Distributed to the U.S. trade and internationally by Penguin Random House Publisher Services.

Berrett-Koehler and the BK logo are registered trademarks of Berrett-Koehler Publishers, Inc.

Printed in the United States.

Berrett-Koehler books are printed on long-lasting acid-free paper. When it is available, we choose paper that has been manufactured by environmentally responsible processes. These may include using trees grown in sustainable forests, incorporating recycled paper, minimizing chlorine in bleaching, or recycling the energy produced at the paper mill.

Library of Congress Cataloging-in-Publication Data
Names: Zheng, Lily, author. | Hansen, Inge (Inge Margrethe), author.
Title: The ethical sellout : maintaining your integrity in the age of
  compromise / Lily Zheng and Inge Hansen.
Description: First edition. | Oakland, CA : Berrett-Koehler Publishers,
  [2019]
Identifiers: LCCN 2019020660 | ISBN 9781523085842 (paperback)
Subjects: LCSH: Integrity. | Conduct of life.
Classification: LCC BJ1533.I58 Z44 2019 | DDC 179/.9--dc23
LC record available at https://lccn.loc.gov/2019020660

FIRST EDITION
25 24 23 22 21 20 19   10 9 8 7 6 5 4 3 2 1

Book producer and editor: PeopleSpeak
Book design and composition: Beverly Butterfield
Cover designer: Irene Morris

To my younger self, who thought she had
to be a perfect activist to be a good one.
I'm glad you were wrong.
Lily

To my parents, in gratitude for
all their love and support.
Inge

Contents

Introduction

When we decided to write this book, we had been working in separate but overlapping spheres for several years. Our work was different in many ways: Inge was a university clinician; Lily was a diversity, equity, and inclusion consultant. What brought us together were stories.

Lily, as an activist, researcher, and consultant, was inundated with stories of all kinds: that of the grassroots organizer fighting for justice, the entry-level employee working to climb up in the workplace, the startup founder grappling with hiring a diverse team. Lily noticed, however, that other stories, beneath the surface, weren't being told. One close friend shared that she wanted to leave the activist community. A research participant nervously described compromising her appearance to avoid discrimination. Some of the people with the strongest identities and most deeply held values seemed also to be struggling most with feelings of fear, apprehension, and self-doubt around the everyday decisions they made. They experienced guilt, shame, and self-blame around their choices yet constantly worked to maintain the impression that they were model members of their communities.

Inge, a clinical psychologist who has worked everywhere from the San Diego LGBT Center to the California prison system and who currently directs student health equity and well-being services at Stanford University, has heard more than her fair share of stories as well in the course of her work. She was struck by the decisions that her clients grappled with the most, which often seemed to be conflicts between who they thought they were supposed to be and who they were becoming. It seemed that over and over, people would come to her office as though seeking permission—or forgiveness—for being themselves. They worried that they were letting down their family or community by seeking their own path, which was confusing in the face of the predominant cultural message: "Be yourself."

We have deeply personal reasons for writing this book as well: namely, that we've both had our own experiences of selling out.

Lily sold out when she decided to work for the same institution that, as a student activist, she had protested. She sold out her own belief in the importance of grassroots change when she started her own for-profit business working with large corporations. And she sells out every day as she tries to create a public-facing persona that balances authenticity and rebelliousness with the respectability she needs to work with her clients.

Inge sells out her queer identity when people assume based on her appearance that she's straight and she doesn't correct them—she gets to be out when it's safe and convenient, and she doesn't have to be when it's not. Similar to Lily, she sold out her activist communities and her own social justice beliefs by working within a well-funded elite institution rather than dedicating her time to supporting the struggling nonprofits that need her more.

Based on our own stories and those we heard from others, we suspected that despite our aversion to the idea of becoming sellouts, all of us nevertheless sell out at some point in our lives. In fact, it seemed likely that most of us sell out in small ways on a regular basis. We wrote this book to answer two questions: "What compels so many of us to sell out?" and "How can we sell out ethically?"

We started this book as a search to find the so-called sellouts in the world. We suspected that after hearing their stories, we would be able to identify "unethical" sellouts from their "ethical" counterparts: those who made selling-out decisions based on necessity rather than greed. We were surprised to find that all the people we spoke with described the same challenges. They worked to find their place within their social and demographic groups, whether racial or religious, professional or political. They faced situations where they were tempted in the moment to sacrifice their beliefs or values for something else, whether for safety, security, personal gain, or other reasons. And overwhelmingly, they struggled with whether they were making the right choice. In other words, we found that the line between ethical and unethical selling out was much blurrier than we had anticipated.

In the first section of this book, we'll share a framework we developed to understand and interpret the many stories we heard. We'll explore the stories of over a dozen people from a colorful range of backgrounds who have all struggled with decisions to sell out, whose stories span contexts from high-tech corporations, elite universities, the US military, and beyond. After each story, we'll unpack the decisions that people made for themselves and discuss what their stories teach us about selling out ethically.

In the second section of this book, we'll pull everything together. We'll revisit our framework and adapt it into a toolkit that all of us can use in our own lives—not to become ethical sellouts but to sell out more ethically.

If you are a young person navigating how your identities and beliefs might color your career and life decisions, this book is for you. If you are middle-aged and seeking personal or professional balance, new meaning, and authenticity, this book is for you. If you are an activist or a person with strong community ties wondering how to live your values given the realities of our current economic and political climate, this book is for you. This book is for all who have ever felt forced to choose between their needs and their values. This book is for those who strive every day to maintain their integrity in the face of constant pressure to compromise.

This book is for you.

Chapter 1

Framing
CHANGE

John formed his first band with his friends when he was sixteen years old. His mother gave him a cheap guitar to support his new hobby, but his family expected (maybe even hoped) that not much would come of it. Music wasn't a real way to make a living, after all. Four years later, John's band was still playing. It had been renamed, gathered some new members, and played regularly at red-light-district clubs around town.

One night, the band's growing underground popularity attracted the attention of a local record-store owner who recognized their untapped mainstream potential. After wooing John and his bandmates with talk of record contracts and stardom, this man was signed on to be their manager. True to his word, he catapulted John's band to success—but at a price. He told them that their underground look would have to go. They had to dress and act differently than they wanted: wear "professional" clothing on stage and tame their stage presence. John resisted the idea but eventually gave in, saying, "I'll wear a bloody balloon if somebody's going to pay me."

The band John Lennon formed, the Beatles, gained international stardom, yet John felt conflicted about how they got there. In a 1971 *Rolling Stone* interview, he stated,

As soon as we made it, we made it, but the edges were knocked off.

You know [our manager] Brian put us in suits and all that, and we made it very, very big. But we sold out, you know. The music was dead before we even went on the theater tour of Britain. . . .

The Beatles music died then, as musicians. That's why we never improved as musicians; we killed ourselves then to make it.[1]

Define "Sellout"

When we first started interviewing the people whose stories appear in this book, we asked each of them to define the word "sellout." Here are a few of the answers:

- "When you sell out, you have nothing left of your 'authentic' self to give."

- "Sacrificing the integrity of your original mission."

- "Compromising your ethics or code of values for money."

People's understanding of what makes a sellout is surprisingly consistent. In fact, it matches up well with Dictionary.com's definition:

> ### sellout
> *noun*
> A person who compromises his or her
> personal values, integrity, or talent, or the like,
> for money or personal advancement.

"Sellout" isn't a word that many think of in neutral terms. Say the word in your head and you might catch yourself injecting a hint of malice in it, a bite of scorn. You'd likely say it the same way you might say "traitor," "poser," or "liar." Start imagining the face of a modern-day sellout and you'll soon see why. You might think of the politician who leaves campaign promises unfulfilled after meeting lobbyists with deep pockets, or the musician who turns their back on their roots to pursue big record deals and corporate sponsorships. You might think of the small-town nobody who strikes it rich and leaves their old friends and communities behind or the activist who backsteps on their radical opinions after gaining celebrity status and joining the establishment.

These kinds of stories tend to be shared with the same moral message: when you betray your communities, your cause, or even your own values, you lose something sacred about yourself. Even if what you've traded your values for isn't money, you've compromised your integrity and become a traitor in the process. We don't want to call ourselves sellouts because, well, we're not traitors.

It's true that we're not all traitors toward others, at least not in a way that is dangerous or damaging. But we are all at times traitors to our own values, beliefs, and identities. The reasons for this are rooted in the economic, social, and political structure of our society. The people we spoke with had some ideas about that as well:

- "Selling out is to some extent inevitable because we live in capitalism and we need money to live. I don't know that it's possible not to sell out. I would say it's about selling out the minimum amount possible to survive."

- "Our society encourages selling out, or this incremental march away from your ideals. We have to be on alert for it. If you're an activist or artist or one of these things that doesn't generate wealth for those who are more powerful, then you are encouraged to find a way to sell your labor to the highest bidder to survive."

More and more signs seemed to suggest that stories of tough choices and uncomfortable compromises are, in fact, universal. We might not all be sellouts. But it seems like all of us, at some point and in some circumstances, sell out.

The Context

We live in a capitalist society. As a consequence, people feel pressure to do what sells to get by, which can impact job choice, how one markets oneself, how one's work is negotiated (e.g., you may be an artist needing to produce work that appeals to the masses), and also what type of lifestyle is affordable (e.g., you may believe in a completely organic diet and cruelty-free clothing and walking to work each day, but you have a Walmart clothing budget and can't afford to live close enough to your work to walk there).

Systems of Oppression

Our society values some types of bodies, identities, and experiences over others. This means that women, LGBTQ+ people, people of color, people with disabilities, the elderly, and people with persecuted systems of faith will not have the same access to opportunity as people with more privileged identities. People who hold one or more marginalized identities can find themselves torn between their loyalty to their community and the freedom and opportunities that come with doing what it takes to get ahead, whether that means distancing from an identity, hiding it, or even using it for profit.

These factors create a cultural context in which selling out in some form is often necessary for survival. If you've ever struggled with tough compromises that are more about safety and getting by than about making it big, you are far from alone.

Suffering in Silence

Despite how commonplace selling out is, you would never guess it because people don't tend to talk about it. Not only that, we tend to go to some lengths to promote the *opposite* narrative: I know who I am, I'm uncompromising in my values, I follow my moral compass in times of struggle, meaningful work matters more than money.

In the 1990s, Deborah Prentice and Dale Miller looked into the culture of alcoholism and drinking at Princeton University. They found that overall, students were largely uncomfortable with the drinking culture on campus yet consistently believed other students to be more comfortable than they were. To "fit in," students would make jokes about drinking, allude to feats of intoxication, and otherwise give the impression that they were just like everyone else—even though students who didn't drink were part of the majority.[2] This phenomenon, called pluralistic ignorance, also describes many people's beliefs about selling out.

Largely because of the stigma surrounding decisions to sell out and the label of "sellout," few people feel able to talk about their real experiences. They worry that by sharing their decisions, they will be mocked and ostracized by their communities and seen as failures. The prevailing assumption is *most people don't sell out or compromise in the way that I did, which makes me a bad person.* As a result, people deal with the intense feelings that accompany a sellout decision in isolation. In the stories we heard, this marginalization and stigma surrounding decisions to sell out led to significant challenges for people in these situations.

The Concepts

We developed two concepts that helped us understand choices to sell out and their aftermath. These concepts, the *impossible choice* and the *moral smoke detector*, illustrate the types of situations that lead to selling out dilemmas, as well as the process by which many of us make moral or ethical decisions.

The Impossible Choice

You make a mistake at work that, if you told your supervisor, would potentially lead to your being fired. Your family is in a tough financial patch, and you can't afford to lose your job.

Your faith community is your home, yet you don't always agree with the members' beliefs. For instance, your pastor has made it very clear that women should be subservient to men. When you make an attempt to gently challenge this assertion, he doubles down on his statement that women must know their place, and the congregation nods along with him.

You're doing groundbreaking research that could change the trajectory of your field in important ways. You just found out that the organization funding your research has white supremacist ties.

We've all had to make choices in our own lives between two or more things that are important to us. Sometimes these things are the identities that make us who we are. Sometimes they are the beliefs and values that we've committed to. Other times, they are the duties and responsibilities we have to our families, communities, and people we care about.

When we imagine the act of selling out, it's easy to project an easy indifference onto the act and assume that those who sell out are heartless people without values or morals. But over the course of our story-collecting journey, we didn't meet anyone like that. We did meet a professional who had to choose between upholding his values and supporting his family, an entrepreneur who had to choose between her racial identity and her career, a professor who had to choose between loyalty to his friend and fulfilling his professional obligations, and many others struggling with painful dilemmas. As the grief, stress, anxiety, and frustration that they expressed to us indicated, these decisions were rarely easy.

We've named the feeling of being forced to choose between two or more things we care deeply about the *impossible choice* to highlight just how challenging such decisions can be. Of course, few "impossible choices" are literally impossible to make. But the struggle that accompanies these decisions, whether they're made after months of consideration or in the heat of the moment, is worthy of attention. We call this conflict the impossible choice in recognition of how difficult it can feel at its worst and in the hopes that we can find gems of insight in the stories we heard that can make these experiences feel a little less impossible.

Compasses and Smoke Detectors

When faced with a dilemma involving your values, you might try to frame the decision with a question: "What does my moral compass say?" That's how most of us think about morality and integrity: as a choice to walk in the direction of our compass or away from it.

But a moral compass isn't an accurate way to talk about how we make decisions. If we really want to get into the weeds of it, humans make decisions through a mix of (some) rational and (mostly) irrational processes. We favor the choices people like us have made before us. Our emotions during the decision process—even if they come from a completely unrelated event—shape our choices. We forget or ignore most of the information we need to make an informed decision. And the role of morality in all this? It's a little more complicated than just pulling out our compass, finding north, and walking in the right direction.

Alan was a young man who was trying to make it as an actor in New York. He'd been getting some work here and there when he was offered a huge opportunity: a lead role in an off-Broadway show. He would be playing a man who pretends to be gay to flirt with his attractive neighbor without risking the ire of her macho boyfriend. "The role was insulting and politically incorrect," he shared with us. "But it was a lead in an off-Broadway play. It was a weekly check. And so I decided to do it."

However, as soon as he started rehearsal, he noticed that something was off. Alan, who was usually very social and talkative, was withdrawing from his fellow cast members. He wasn't socializing nearly as much as he usually did. And that wasn't all: "I was having trouble learning my lines," he recalled, "which was purely psychological because I'm one of the fastest studies I know. I had no appetite. I had a pain in my stomach all week. My brain was telling me that something was not right, and my heart was too." After five days of feeling this way, Alan called the stage manager and let him know he couldn't go through with playing the role. Immediately, the pain in his stomach disappeared. He felt famished for the first time after barely eating all week. He reflected: "My north star for the rest of my career was, 'How does it feel in the pit of your stomach? Does it feel right, or does it not feel right?'"

Like Alan, many people described experiences of making a decision that felt uneventful or mundane, only to be gripped with feelings of guilt, shame, anger, or pain soon afterward. We decided to give this concept a name: the *moral smoke detector*. Smoke detectors aren't sophisticated.

They'll tell you when you've messed up and something's on fire but not much else. And even when they are trying to discern an actual house fire from harmless cooking smoke, they are famously inaccurate and oversensitive. When we feel strong emotions like guilt or shame after a decision, that can often be a signal for us to revisit and reflect on the choice that triggered these emotions. The smoke detector can be a sign that we made a choice out of line with our values—or just that we have an overly sensitive alarm system.

Smoke detectors and compasses work hand in hand as we grow up. When you were young, did you ever get in trouble for breaking your parents' rules or act in a way that someone you respected disapproved of? As we set off our moral smoke detectors, we learn about our own moral beliefs. Maybe getting reprimanded by your teacher never stresses you out, but forgetting about a personal commitment makes you feel awful. Maybe you readily game the system to get ahead without batting an eye, but you become paralyzed with anxiety when forced to lie. Over time, as we clarify our strongest moral beliefs, our moral compass is formed. Alan, after stepping down from the role, vowed to rely on his gut feeling in the future—adapting what he learned from his moral smoke detector to adjust his moral compass. The mistake that many of us make is to assume that with time, our moral smoke detectors will stop going off as often and eventually stop altogether. Not so. The interplay of smoke detector and compass continues for our entire lives.

Assembling the Parts

If we put all these factors together, we find ourselves with the following:

1. An economic, social, and political system that makes selling-out dilemmas almost inevitable

2. A tendency to believe we are alone when we grapple with these dilemmas

3. Conflicts between our values, beliefs, duties, and obligations that can be so challenging we refer to them as "impossible choices"

4. A somewhat faulty, unreliable system for guiding us through these ethical dilemmas, which often lets us know we've made a mistake only after the fact

On the surface, selling out appears to be a selfish act, a breach of good values. The truth is that it does harm to view selling out simply as a failure of moral character, rather than nuanced decision-making in the context of a seemingly impossible choice.

With this in mind, we arrived at the question that would inform the rest of our book: How do you sell out ethically?

It Takes CHANGE

We realized quickly that there was no easy "five-step plan" to sell out ethically. Yet it was clear that some people feel far more comfortable about their decisions and their process for making them than others do. We realized that selling out ethically involved skills that could be practiced. We eventually distilled from these stories six individual skills that better equip individuals to sell out ethically.

Skill 1: Compassion

Our culture teaches us that selling out is greedy, uncaring, and selfish, but in reality, those who sell out can be the opposite: overly self-critical and self-judgmental. The first skill of selling out ethically is *compassion*, both for yourself and others. Understanding that selling-out decisions are both difficult and universal allows you to fight isolation, guilt, and shame and more resiliently weather the hardship of even the most impossible of choices.

Skill 2: Honesty

Our minds are skilled at making uncomfortable situations disappear, but the path to selling out ethically requires self-awareness. The second skill of selling out ethically is *honesty*, fighting your own cognitive distortions and rationalizations to understand who you are and why you make the choices you make. Being honest with yourself allows you to understand how and why you do what you do and approach your decisions with clarity rather than confusion.

Skill 3: Accountability

Who and what are we responsible for? Every action has an impact, and regardless of our intentions, the impacts on ourselves and those around us are ours to own. The third skill of selling out ethically is *accountability*, taking responsibility for the outcomes of your decisions to sell out, whether good or bad. Practicing accountability allows you to evaluate the impact of your choices and make things right if needed.

Skill 4: Nuance

The world isn't a simple place, and neither are the ideas in it. Oftentimes, existing in the world requires the resilience, foresight, and intuition to navigate uncertainty and ambiguity. The fourth skill of selling out ethically is *nuance*, recognizing that there's no one "right" way to be or do anything and that your individual circumstances are unique. No one is perfect or pure—the real work happens in the gray areas. Recognizing nuance means understanding the full context behind your choices, and challenging black-and-white thinking in your decision-making.

Skill 5: Growth

We get new opportunities to sell out all the time, opportunities to make mistakes and learn from them. Even when we feel comfortable, it's important not to be static. The fifth skill of selling out ethically is *growth,* using conflict and discomfort as learning moments to reaffirm your values and beliefs, fight isolation, and create new meaning. Embracing growth allows you to be more resilient when challenges arise and approach failure with humility and grace rather than fear.

Skill 6: Exploration

Selling out ethically isn't a one-time achievement but a way of living life actively, continually questioning and renegotiating the world around you. The best antidote to stagnation, inflexibility, and settling is a commitment to the last skill of selling out ethically: *exploration,* expressing curiosity and wonder as you go through life. Committing to exploration allows you to stay engaged with a changing world and welcome your own changes throughout your life span.

The first letters of these six skills spell out CHANGE (a feat that took far too long on thesaurus.com)—because for all of us, making the jump from selling out to selling out ethically requires change. Each of these skills represents a path toward navigating compromise and maintaining our integrity along the way. Used wisely in conjunction with each other, these skills can help you better approach an impossible choice and center yourself after the decision is made. We will start by sharing selling-out stories using this framework as a lens and then discuss the framework extensively in the latter half of the book.

The Stories

Unfortunately, we don't happen to know either of the surviving Beatles members or any high-ranking politicians. We had a hunch, though, that we could find selling-out stories just about anywhere—and we were right. Over many months, we spoke with dozens of people across the country to hear their stories and see if our idea of what selling out looked like resembled theirs. Some people volunteered to speak with us once they learned about our project; others we found via social media and other means. Two people were public figures whose stories we compiled via their own writings and public statements. We spoke with self-identified sellouts and those who vehemently denounced the label. We spoke with individuals at the start of their journeys and those nearing the end. And we learned that people who sell out are a pretty diverse bunch. They are students and office managers, conservatives and liberals, artists and businesspeople. They span race, gender, income level, religion, ability status, and nationality.

As you read these stories, we hope that you can withhold your judgment of the choices people made, even for just a little while. To write this book, we trained ourselves to focus not on the right or wrong of people's choices but on how and why they made these decisions. Do we have our own personal feelings about how people handled their dilemmas? Of course. But we chose these stories for our book not as parables to illustrate perfect or problematic behavior but as genuine and at times messy examples of how and why people sell out. These stories reflect ethical dilemmas, and we're presenting them to you because we want you to explore the gray spaces experienced by the participants. We recommend that as you engage with these stories, you try your best to focus not on the *what* of people's choices but on the *how* and *why*.

Chapter 2

The Stranger in the Mirror

None of us get to choose our genetics. However, the truth is that some of us are handed challenges that will make our lives more difficult right from the beginning: we hold an identity or characteristic that makes it harder to function the way we'd like or that our society treats as inferior. In those cases, we often find ourselves in a place of reckoning where we may either move toward embracing our full selves despite the challenges or try to change or disown parts of ourselves.

The stories in this chapter are from people who chose the former option: to love themselves just as they are and find peace with the negative messages they received from others. However, just when they thought they had reached a solid place of self-acceptance, something happened that led them to question everything and make different choices.

Sophie

Sophie, who uses she/her pronouns, wondered for the fifth time that week if she should follow through with her bariatric surgery. The pale-skinned, red-haired woman debated whether the procedure, which promised a slew of benefits to her health, was worth the cost. Up until recently, Sophie— who proudly identified as fat—would have never considered a procedure like this. But circumstances had changed.

The daughter of blue-collar parents in Florida, Sophie had been a fat child and a fat teenager. In fact, she had been fat for as long as she could remember, a reality that her family seemed determined to remedy. For more than a decade, Sophie's day-to-day life was punctuated by endless diets, scales, and punishments for failing to lose weight. "I'm a good kid, I get good grades, I don't get in trouble, what's so wrong with me?" Sophie recalled saying through tears to her mom. Sophie was in her teens and had just come back from the local weight-loss clinic, where a doctor had put staples in Sophie's ears to curb her appetite. Her mom started crying as well. "There's nothing wrong with you," she said. "I just know how hard it's gonna be if you don't lose weight."

Whether as the butt of jokes, objects of scorn, or targets for discrimination, fat people in America endure pervasive mistreatment.[1] The stigma of being fat has real costs: Americans spend more on dieting every year than on video games or movies. Forty-five percent of all adults say they think about their weight some or all of the time.[2] Much of the discrimination fat people face comes from their own family members, who push diets, verbal abuse, and discipline onto their larger children. Doctors, rather than address larger individuals' health, frequently discriminate against their weight. Study after study finds that when a patient is fat, regardless of the real issue, doctors are less likely to provide a diagnosis beyond the two words "lose weight."[3]

In college, Sophie learned a different way to interact with her body. Away from her parents and their army of doctors, she met people of all shapes and sizes who were happy with their bodies. For the first time, Sophie wondered if her body was okay the way it was, if she could even be desirable to other people. Her partners convinced her that that must be true. Sophie started calling herself fat but as a point of pride, not shame.

"It's odd reframing these messages you've gotten your whole life about how there's something wrong with you," she said, "when there's nothing wrong with me. I'm totally fine as I am." Fatphobia was the problem; prejudice was the problem—not her and not her body. Her relationship to food and her relationship to her appearance and her weight had been influenced by others' expectations for her. Now, she would take her body back into her own hands.

"I asked myself, 'What really is *my* relationship to food and where do *I* want to make changes for myself as opposed to what other people want?'"

Her journey to self-acceptance had been breathtaking, but at the moment, Sophie was in her room grappling with some news. Her latest checkup revealed the same results as her last: high blood pressure, arthritis in both knees, and prediabetes. Dieting and exercise alone hadn't helped, and her doctor had suggested she consider bariatric surgery to lose weight. It was even covered by her insurance—all she needed to do was say yes.

The situation felt tremendously unfair to Sophie. She had just come to a place of acceptance of her body and her identity as a woman of size. She didn't want to succumb to all the messages she'd heard throughout her life that something was wrong with her due to her weight or give her parents any ammunition for an "I told you so." While she understood that many of the negative messages she'd previously heard about being fat came from a place of prejudice and false assumptions, she was now dealing with a real-life health consequence related to her weight. If she didn't go for the surgery, the alternative was almost certainly diabetes.

"It was really starting to freak me out," Sophie admitted, and she made her choice. She would undergo gastric bypass surgery—not out of shame but for her health. Six months later, with a diet plan and a support program, Sophie came out of surgery with no major complications. Her weight dropped soon afterward into a range that lowered her risk for diabetes and other health concerns, and her doctor was satisfied.

Sophie, however, was grieving. She had lost more than pounds of weight: the surgery had taken away her relationship with her body too:

> I did all this work over all these years and got to this place where I have a great life and relationships and great sex and things that I grew up thinking I would never have because I was fat. I was getting really comfortable with that and getting to a point where I could say, "That's their problem." To then have my body be so different and have to figure out my relationship with my body again and my relationship with food, it was a huge shift, and it's not something I thought I would ever have to do again.

That was several years ago. Now Sophie has no regrets about the decision she made but still hasn't fully made peace with it. "I still judge myself for having done it," she admits. "It doesn't feel like a battle, just an ongoing process. I think it's impossible not to internalize on some level that feeling that there was something wrong with me. Like there's a moral shortcoming for being fat. And if I could just get myself together, if I could just have enough will-power, if I could be better and stronger, I could have lost enough weight to no longer be prediabetic and not have to do surgery."

Sophie still hashes out these questions with a small community of others who have received gastric bypasses. One of the biggest questions they grappled with is, "Am I still fat?" For them, fat had become an identity and not simply a matter of size. "It's a struggle," Sophie reflected. "Now it's no longer obviously visible that being fat is part of who I am. You feel like you left your people behind. A part of me feels like I left behind a part of me. It feels like I stepped outside the community and the door closed behind me."

Julia

Julia, a Jewish woman in her twenties who uses she/her pronouns, has thick brown hair and an easy laugh. She's lived with a significant neuromuscular disability her whole life, which has resulted in severe mobility issues and the need to rely on an attendant most hours of the day.

> Traditional medical models perceive disabilities as impairments that exist within an individual. The solution therefore is to cure or prevent the impairment or alleviate its impact through treatment. The social model of disability considers barriers to access the primary issue. The solution is to address inaccessible environments, discrimination and prejudice, and problematic organizational practices and procedures.[4]

Much like Sophie and her weight, Julia had originally understood her disability from a medical model standpoint: a problem to be fixed and a source of shame. She remembers being a poster child for a telethon designed to raise money to prevent children from being born with disabilities and then realizing later that the goal of such telethons was to prevent people like her from being born. The message to her was clear: she was a burden to society.

Like Sophie, Julia was exposed to new ways of thinking in college. She began to see that her disability wasn't the problem: society's failure to accommodate it and treat her with respect was.

Through this new lens, Julia came to see ableism, not her disability, as the real issue. "It was one of the most liberating experiences of my life," Julia said. "It totally changed my work and what I want to do with my life." She was inspired to become a disability rights activist. She began attending conferences and connecting with others who shared her disability. She even began making a documentary film about living with her disability to help others better understand her experience.

Julia's disability is progressive, meaning that with each passing year she could lose functioning. She said, "When you have a progressive disability, as soon as you lose a function, it's terrifying and it seems impossible to live your life the way you were with the new parameters. But after a surprisingly short amount of time, you adjust and it's fine and you forget that life was any different or what your body was able to do before. It just seems like it was like this always."

Julia's disability seemed to progress rapidly in her twenties, and shortly after finishing college, Julia was faced with the possibility that despite her Ivy League education and passion for social justice, she might never be able to reach her ambitious career goals.

Just then, a new treatment was approved by the US Food and Drug Administration that would not only stop the progression of Julia's disability but reverse it to a degree. Many of her able-bodied friends and family saw this as a no-brainer: with this treatment, Julia could likely live longer, have a better quality of life, and fulfill her career aspirations. However, to Julia, taking this treatment would mean renouncing her deeply held belief that disabilities are to be embraced, not "fixed." "I've worked so hard to get to a place where I don't see myself as a deficient human being due to my disability," she said. "If I take this treatment, it will be like saying that I was lying to myself and to the disability community all along, that I was all for self-acceptance until there was an alternative option."

She worried that taking the treatment would be a betrayal of her community and a validation of ableism: "If I want to stop the progression of my disability, if I don't want to become more disabled and maybe I do want to get some function back and become more able-bodied, it felt like I was being a hypocrite and that I was selling out to the able-bodied majority."

Julia found herself with what felt like an impossible choice. Should she get the treatment and lose her identity as a proud disability rights activist, potentially forsaking others who see her as a role model and inspiration? Or should she refuse the treatment and face the inevitable decline in physical function and its personal and professional consequences?

Julia waited, unable to stomach the idea of making a choice she saw as necessary but selfish. But as she waited, she was surprised by the support of friends, including friends with disabilities, who told her that they understood her hesitation but that no one was expecting her to martyr herself for a cause. "No one is going to look back and say, 'Oh she did the right thing and it was a good thing that she died young,'" she repeated to us. Julia felt she would have been making an important statement by refusing the treatment but that the impact of her statement would be relatively small, especially when compared to the physical consequences of refusing treatment. Ultimately, Julia said, nearly everyone she knows with her disability did go for the treatment.

Now in her first year of graduate school, Julia is on her way to fulfilling her personal and professional goals as she undergoes the treatment. "I've had a recurring thought: I couldn't do this without it. I couldn't do grad school the way I'm currently doing it without having done the treatment," she reflected. "It was just a sad realization to have because I don't like thinking that I couldn't live my life how I want to if I had the natural course of my body's progression."

Her worst fears never materialized. Julia is still a part of the disability community and continues to feel loved and welcomed by her friends within it, even as she works through her own feelings. She continues to identify as a disability rights activist. Since Julia's treatment is ongoing, she's never able to look away from her decision, and regaining functions she had already come to terms with losing forever is a continual adjustment. "I still feel like I was a hypocrite and that I sold out to the able-bodied majority," she admitted, but ultimately, she does not regret her decision. With the support of her community, she will keep adapting and moving forward—lessons her disability has already taught her well.

Reflection

Sophie's and Julia's stories represent many things, including adjusting to adversity, grappling with loss, and engaging with community. What we took away from these lessons was that Sophie and Julia were able to strengthen their resilience through practicing *compassion*. Sophie felt like her prediabetes was a slap in the face to her body positivity. Yet after she went through her surgery, she put forward genuine effort to hold on to the healthy relationship she had developed with her body. The support group she speaks to even today continues to be a space of shared compassion among others with similar experiences.

Julia struggled with compassion at first. The fact that she was even willing to consider a procedure that she had just learned about, to undo a part of her she had spent her entire life coming to terms with, felt already like a betrayal. Julia's fellow disability community members provided a reality check and helped Julia practice compassion for herself. They were able to help her think about the decision without self-judgment.

Healing Is a Moving Target

Sophie and Julia struggled with what it meant to be fat and to have a disability, respectively. The challenges they faced were due only in part to inherent physical challenges, such as health problems or lack of function. A significant portion of their experiences were shaped by cultural and societal perceptions and stigma: both were given the message that their bodies were problematic because they varied from what our culture views as attractive and valuable. Sophie was subjected to constant forced diets and messages that she would never find a partner, whereas Julia was exposed to a medical model of disability that taught her that she was a charity case and that her disability was a problem to be fixed.

But neither Sophie nor Julia wanted to change who she was. Instead, both women embraced a different way of viewing their bodies: not as unruly battlegrounds to conquer but as objects worthy of love and acceptance just as they were. They rejected the medical models that saw their fatness or disability as a problem and adopted the "social model," a term advocates use to describe understanding how many of the challenges that fat people or disabled people face stem from society and not individual deficits. Both Sophie and Julia found communities that shared identities like theirs and started on what felt like an upward path free of shame and self-hate. And it worked. It took time, but they both made peace with the identities that others had for so long blamed them for having.

This made the choice to give them up much more difficult. Had Sophie been pushed into a gastric bypass by her mom when she believed that her body was the problem, it might have felt like the obvious answer. Had Julia had a choice to undo her disability when she still saw it as a pure liability, it might have felt much easier. But making the choice when they did, at a point when they were happy and content with their identities, was hard. Even harder was dealing with the aftermath of their choices, as Sophie's health risks decreased and Julia's disability reversed but they both struggled with the identities that had brought them pride and community.

Selling out means new advantages (no one would do it otherwise!) that are inevitably mixed with real loss. As a result of their decisions, Sophie and Julia found themselves in murky worlds: what does it mean to be a formerly fat person or someone with a partially reversed disability? Yet Sophie and Julia both gained a degree of societal power through these identity transformations. As a result, they felt relief—and perhaps just as much guilt regarding what they had done to avoid the outcomes they dreaded. They wondered, Is it okay to accept or even appreciate the benefits of a choice that feels like a shortcut to privilege?

We may have spent years coming to terms with our own identities: our race, gender, class, religion, social group, nationality, ability status, or size. We may have faced adversity and transformed what society sees as a deficit into our foundation and the core of our strength, like Sophie and Julie did. You've done this yourself. Think of some aspect of yourself that you used to see as negative but now no longer do. What was your own process like?

What happens when a lost cause gets renewed hope? When something we believed to be permanent becomes optional? Even before we've made a choice, just knowing that things were not how we believed them to be almost always disrupts our natural processes of grief, loss, and healing around what it means to be ourselves in this world. On the surface, the choice can seem obvious (who wouldn't want to be richer, thinner, healthier, etc.?), but we often find that aspects of our being can't be shed as easily as clothing. We're not just letting go of an identity—we're letting go of the real and symbolic value that identity meant to us and at least outwardly disavowing what we spent so long to build.

After such a transition, we find ourselves asking, Who am I without this thing I was cursing just days ago? Who are my people and who is my community now? Who am I without this familiar struggle? This change in social identity can create an experience of living in two worlds at once: the former world, which shaped us, and the new world, which doesn't feel fully ours yet and may not ever. The trouble with living in two worlds, of course, is that neither one may feel like home. In the weeks and months after making such a choice, it's tempting to wonder, Was this really worth the cost?

For many of us, the person we are today is a collection of the struggles we have overcome.

Community: Source of Refuge or Rejection?

We call the difficult decisions people make impossible choices because at some time they truly do feel impossible. Making these decisions on your own is even harder. For most of us, this isolation is a self-imposed situation. We have communities who can support us, whether social groups we're a part of, loved ones, family, or trusted friends. Sometimes all we have to do is remember that they exist and convince ourselves that they can and want to help.

Community is powerful. It can help us process the choices we made, like Sophie's support group did. It can serve as a sounding board for our feelings and give us an outlet to process our thoughts out loud. And, like Julia's friends did, community can help us reframe impossible decisions in more compassionate ways that start to feel less terrifying and more manageable. Julia believed that if she pursued treatment, she would be trading functionality for her identity as a person with a disability, her credibility as an advocate, and the trust her community held in her. Her friends, themselves disability advocates, firmly but kindly challenged those self-critical ideas. They stressed in the clearest of terms that Julia could receive treatment and still be a member of her community, that she could and should still advocate, and that her friends would stay her friends. The impossible decision, after her community's help, seemed much less impossible.

Yet one's community can be a source of pain just as much as a source of support. Sophie and Julia were fortunate, but many people find themselves isolated following an impossible choice. Sometimes this is a person's own doing: the fear of being shamed or rejected following a sellout decision or the concern about not belonging in one's original community anymore can lead a person to close off from others. Other times, the community holds a person under suspicion after such a choice is made, especially when the choice results in increased privilege or upward mobility.

Inge has a friend named Sandra, a Black woman who was raised by a family of modest means and eventually went on to become an esteemed faculty member at an elite university. With each new success she has, every promotion and every new board she is elected to, her family responds the same way. Instead of saying "Congratulations!" or "That's wonderful!" they say, "Stay grounded" or "Don't get too big a head now." This response has always been hurtful to Sandra, who just wants to feel her parents are proud of her. They likely *are* proud of her, but looming larger than that pride is the fear that she'll eventually become so big (or bigheaded) that she'll lose her connection to where she came from.

Sandra is far from alone in her experience. In *Hillbilly Elegy*, J. D. Vance's autobiographical account of the lives of poor white families from Appalachia, he spoke of what happened when his grandparents moved to Ohio to escape poverty:

> A remarkable stigma is attached to people who left the hills of Kentucky for a better life. Hillbillies have a phrase—"too big for your britches"—to describe those who think they're better than the stock they came from. For a long time after my grandparents came to Ohio, they heard exactly that phrase from people back home. The sense that they had abandoned their families was acute, and it was expected that, whatever their responsibilities, they would return home regularly.[5]

Not only were Vance's grandparents subject to criticism and pressure from the folks back home, they received the same from their new neighbors as well. The white middle class of Ohio deeply disapproved of the culture and customs of these Appalachian migrants, possibly because they disrupted local assumptions about how white people appeared, spoke, and behaved.

Sandra and Vance's grandparents found themselves in a catch-22 familiar to many upwardly mobile people from marginalized backgrounds: held with suspicion by their original communities but not fully welcomed into their new ones.

At first glance, understanding why one's community would react in such a way when one of their own is taking a shot at a better life may be difficult. Shouldn't Sandra's and Vance's people be happy for them? The answer is a painful history lesson.

Our past is packed with stories of people who betrayed their communities. While these stories occur irrespective of race, class, and other identities, the betrayal cuts the deepest when it comes from within a community that is already marginalized.

Trans people, cross-dressers, gender rebels, and radical leftists led the LGBTQ+ movement in its early days. Years later, they were pushed aside by the more privileged members of their own community who wanted to disassociate "respectable" gay and lesbian people from the "deviant" bisexual and transgender members of the movement.[6]

William O'Neal, a Black Panther Party member entrusted with keys to Panther headquarters and safe houses, served as an informant to the FBI. His actions led to the extrajudicial murder of Black Panther leader Fred Hampton and the subsequent decline of the Black Panther Party.[7]

These stories and others like them play a surprising role in why many individuals face backlash from their communities when they make decisions around selling out. These are communities that have constantly been under attack from outsiders, communities that rely heavily on in-group solidarity to ward off infiltration and betrayal.

If you're from such a community, make a decision to compromise your identity or your values for gain and you might be seen as less trustworthy. Sure, you're no William O'Neal—but the distrust, the belief that you're "too good" for the community, and the suspicion that you'll use your power for harm still lingers. Sell out and people might ask, "Where do your allegiances now lie?" If people's circumstances change, will they still identify with where they came from? Or will they step out when it becomes inconvenient and leave their community behind?

One of our participants pointed out that people with marginalized identities have a much higher standard for not selling out than people without them:

> Looking at it from the other perspective, why not sell out? Why is it a question of integrity or morality for marginalized people or people of color? Why is that even a thing? Like, why can't Omarosa have her ideas and still be Black? Or Kanye West have his ideas and still be Black?

For instance, if Julia had been able-bodied, she never would have been saddled with her selling-out dilemma to begin with nor the terrible guilt that she felt following her decision. People with disabilities are expected to show up for the disabled community in the way that able-bodied people are not, and the same is true for people of color, LGBTQ+ folks, women, people from low-income backgrounds, and so on.

As a result of these expectations, people with marginalized identities are often made to hold far more community responsibility for their choices compared to people with privileged identities. These expectations can be an unfair burden. Yet they can also result in vibrant and powerful forms of support, advocacy, and community created around mutual responsibility. Without these expectations, these communities might very well be smaller, weaker, or non-existent.

These complicated histories mean that for people who are members of marginalized communities, impossible choices are made that much harder. Individuals questioning whether they should compromise must also consider all these complicated realities about their communities and the impact of their individual decisions.

Chapter 3

In and out
of the Closet

Not everyone contemplates changing an identity for good, but what if it's only for a day or a month? In societies around the world, we're inundated with the idea that living our best lives is living our most authentic lives.[1] We ought to do what we want, love whom we want, and be unapologetically ourselves to make our own way forward. But discrimination and prejudice can cast a shadow on that sunny outlook. For the gay man living in a homophobic neighborhood, the first-generation student in an elite university, or the Muslim person in a rural Christian town, authenticity becomes a more complicated idea. People are constantly navigating the societal advantages and disadvantages of their identities whether they involve race, gender, sexuality, age, ability status, or other markers.

In some cases, people have decided that the disadvantages associated with expressing their identity are so great that they need to hide that identity from others. One way in which we do this is by refusing to disclose our identity or pretending to be another identity. We might mark "decline to state" instead of "female" on surveys or say "Christian" instead of "Jewish" or "Buddhist" when others ask our religion.

Everyone makes decisions, conscious or not, about what aspects of self to express in what situations. The people you'll meet in this chapter are no different. In this chapter, we'll learn from people who made the choice to suppress or hide an important part of themselves and how that decision impacted them.

Tanisha

If she changed her name to sound less Black, would her business do better?

Even the thought felt traitorous. Tanisha, an Afro-Latinx woman and born-and-bred New Yorker who uses she/her pronouns, was raised to take pride in her race. "I was Black, first and always," she said. "It was this foundation of Blackness that stood with me when interacting in mixed spaces. It led me to attend a historically Black college." But despite her upbringing and pride in her racial identity, Tanisha held a secret: she couldn't shake the idea that being Black was a disadvantage in the world.

"I was programmed by society," she told us. "No matter how many Black history classes or homecomings I attended, I didn't believe that Black people could thrive as business owners or high-ranking professionals in the communications industry unless they compromised."

In 2004, economists Marianne Bertrand and Sendhil Mullainathan published the results of their game-changing research, "Are Emily and Greg More Employable Than Lakisha and Jamal? A Field Experiment on Labor Market Discrimination."[2] This study, which has since been cited thousands of times, revealed that simply changing the name on a résumé from a white name to a Black name reduced callbacks by 30 percent. Just to close that gap, a résumé with a Black name had to show eight years of additional job experience than the résumé with the white name.

Tanisha held this belief for two reasons. The first was that she had a dearth of professional role models. While Black women make up 8 percent of the private sector workforce, they make up only 1.5 percent of senior-level executives. (White men make up 33 percent of the workforce but 63 percent of executive-level positions.)[3] The second was that she held no delusions about the reality of discrimination in the field, discrimination against Black people not on the basis of their work or dedication but based on their Blackness alone. "I thought 'Tanisha' sounded too Black," she acknowledged. "People with ghetto-sounding names don't get as far ahead due to perceptions of what they can provide. If the one thing holding me back is a name, then why not change that name?"

When Tanisha started the Rebelle Agency, a public relations and communications business, she opted to use her middle name, Dariana, which felt more racially ambiguous. But she did so defiantly, recognizing both her desire to avoid discrimination and her unwillingness to pretend to be white. "I didn't change my name to Kate," she pointed out. "I wasn't going to completely change my identity. I just wanted to prolong the game a bit longer." And prolong the game she did. To prevent potential clients from confirming her Black identity, she removed all pictures of herself from her websites, business media, and printed materials, leaving only the name Dariana to identify her by.

"Dariana" would be the name she used for six years, but it did not offer her the ease and advantages she had hoped for. Friends who had known her before frequently slipped up and used "Tanisha," and even when they used "Dariana," it was uncomfortable. "I winced whenever anyone else adopted it because it was a constant reminder of my inner conflict," Tanisha reflected. Her business hadn't failed—but the name change hadn't catapulted her into huge success either.

After delivering a big talk at her alma mater on authenticity and success, Tanisha felt a flash of insight:

> I did the talk, I was killin' it, but afterward I felt this *gorilla* on my back. How can you speak so eloquently about authenticity and how it leads to success and that the only way that you could be successful is if you're authentic, and you're literally rolling around with your middle name because you were too afraid to use your first name?

The hypocrisy of the last six years stared her in the face, and Tanisha finally relented. "What am I really afraid of?" she asked herself. "If people don't want to work with me because I'm Black, then I don't want to work with them." Tanisha decided, "F- this. I'm going back to my first name!" So that's what she did.

Looking back, Tanisha has no regrets over changing her name to Dariana and back again. "It was a part of my never-ending quest to find myself," she said, "And getting comfortable with my name was a major leg of that quest." In the end, Tanisha feels she had to dismiss her name to learn to love it.

Shyen

What does it mean to hide who you are for the sake of your career? Shyen, a transgender woman who uses they/them and also she/her pronouns, had grappled with this question for much of their adult life. Growing up in a Southeast Asian country, Shyen was acutely aware of the prejudice and scrutiny they would face from their family, employer, and even the government if they publicly challenged gender norms. But for the moment, they were far away from their home country, sitting in a dorm room at an Ivy League university.

As is the case for many soon-to-be graduates, one of Shyen's biggest questions was, "What will I do after college?" Professionally, Shyen had a clear path in front of them: one year in their home country working for the government, graduate school in the United States, and five more years with the government. These were the terms of the scholarship Shyen had received for their education, and for the most part, Shyen was fine with this arrangement. They were more concerned with how to negotiate their gender identity during these years.

In a perfect world, Shyen would present themselves as "tomboy femme," wearing androgynous versions of women's clothing. They would be visibly gender-nonconforming and challenge other people's perceptions of gender. But being openly trans and visibly gender-nonconforming was a big commitment, whether they were in the United States or in their home country. Authenticity would come at a cost.

In the United States, while their university and some employers could provide safe environments to be authentic, they worried about confrontation outside these environments in the form of street harassment, sexual assault, and violent crime. In their home country, while violence was far less ubiquitous, they worried about the lack of legal protections for transgender and gender-nonconforming people and that their employer wouldn't understand their identity.

"Am I ready to be out about who I am to my employer, given that I'm only going to be here a year?" they wondered. "My decision in the end was that it felt too risky and too complicated to do that. I'll just deal with this. It's just a year. I can deal with this."

Luckily, they had prepared for this choice. While in the States, they chose to undergo medical transition at a slower pace—partially to appear more androgynous and partially also to avoid any large changes that would raise suspicion

Southeast Asia has a long and rich transgender history that often is overlooked by scholars. Gender plurality in Southeast Asian societies was vilified by colonial powers that tried to impose rigid gender norms and roles onto what they viewed as "gender-nonconforming" communities. While these countries today have much progress to make on LGBTQ+ inclusivity, many also treat LGBTQ+ communities in ways that the United States, Europe, and other "Western" countries trail behind on. For example, governments in some countries, such as Thailand and Singapore, provide support for medical transition and transgender health care.[4]

from their family or employer back home.[5] Shyen was now about to start their new government job as an academic and researcher. With only their shoulder-length hair to indicate any potential gender-nonconformity, Shyen went to work. "I went back in the closet again," they told us.

Being a closeted trans academic was a strategic choice to invest in a long-term professional career over short-term authenticity. Yet this compromise didn't come easily.

A lot of my life has been trying to reconcile my radical beliefs about how society could and should be with how I actually live my life, which feels very much like respectability politics. I compare myself to other trans people who are fighting out there on the streets. I get this feeling of survivor's guilt: why am I so lucky that I'm not forced into doing sex work and instead going down this path of "becoming a scholar"?

Not only does hiding their identity for their career make them feel inauthentic, but it also forces them to back off from the advocacy they care so much about. "If you take a government scholarship, you're expected to go by the rules," Shyen explained. They recall one case where a trans student from their high school was forced to conform to her school's dress code standard for boys rather than girls. "That made me really angry," Shyen recalls. They reached out and offered to rally young alumni of the school and raise a fuss on the student's behalf but found themselves hesitating. "I didn't ever get around to doing that. Partly she didn't want it, but also what happened was that I kept putting it off. It was scary putting my name out there as supportive of her because I wasn't out. I wasn't sure I was willing to bear public scrutiny." Eventually, time passed and it was too late. The trans student dropped out.

Ultimately, despite the difficulties that accompany Shyen's compromise, they believe they made the right choice. "The decision I've made is that it's worth it to bide my time," they said, but were nevertheless relieved to be holding out only temporarily. "I know after this much time living in my home country that this compromise is really not sustainable for me. I'll be starting graduate school in a liberal city in the United States soon, and there I know I can be out as trans. It'll be a huge relief when I start."

In the meantime, Shyen has been maintaining their identity as best they can. "Given these confines, I try to live in a way that I don't give up all of myself." Part of how they do this is by maintaining an online presence as an out trans woman. "I have this hope of being able to be that inspiration for other younger trans people in my home country, both now and hopefully in the future as an openly transgender academic," they shared. "That does bring me a lot of joy, and it has already happened for people who have friended me on social media. That's been really meaningful, knowing that even though I'm not totally out, the degree to which I'm out on social media has already helped people live more authentically." And in the office, Shyen has been slowly pushing their attire toward the androgynous side. "I presented as more conventionally masculine at the start. It's only after I started talking in meetings more and showing that I'm a competent researcher that I started dressing more unconventionally." Despite the difficulty of walking the fine line between authenticity and safety at work, Shyen feels like they're surviving as best they can and perhaps subtly shifting people's notions of gender while they're at it.

"People definitely notice," they admitted with a hint of pride. "They can't not."

Reflection

We saw Tanisha's and Shyen's experiences as strong examples of *growth* and *nuance*, respectively. Tanisha compromised her identity as a Black woman when she vowed to take on a more ambiguous name and remove pictures of herself from her website. We were struck not only by her compromise but her experience of realizing her own double standards. Tanisha's ability to learn from her compromise was one of the most poignant examples of growth we saw.

Shyen's seemingly simple decision to hide their identity belied a deceptively complicated calculus. The way in which Shyen simultaneously handled huge questions of identity, authenticity, safety, and strategy in making their choice struck us as a powerful example of nuanced decision-making with no right answer.

Passing to Survive

Sometimes it's not possible to hide an aspect of your identity. See someone and you'll immediately notice the color of their skin. Listen to anyone over the phone and you'll find yourself assuming their gender based on the voice you hear. But other times, we are able to hide some aspect of ourselves to "pass" as something we're not. Tanisha could delay clients' biases by choosing a less Black name and removing her image from her website to appear ethnically ambiguous. Shyen could wear clothing that didn't raise too many questions about their gender.

Passing isn't a new idea. American history is full of people who consciously passed as racially ambiguous or white as a route to avoid racial discrimination and violence.[6] But even as racial passing has become less prominent in an increasingly multiracial America, plenty of other forms of passing have risen to take its place. Many authors, including J. K. Rowling of Harry Potter fame, published under a gender-ambiguous pen name to dodge sexism.[7]

Passing is hardest when it requires a constant effort to hide a secret. Tanisha ran up against this challenge and arguably failed: when she tried to adopt the name "Dariana" full-time, her friends either could not remember the new name or never took it seriously. Neither Tanisha nor Shyen sought to become something they were not over the long run. Tanisha's persona was Dariana, a racially ambiguous woman who with any luck wouldn't be a target for racism. Shyen's persona was a man with long hair who with any luck wouldn't be a target for transphobia. For Tanisha, it was about business success. For Shyen, it was about the viability of a future career in a conservative country.

Shyen's double life required more than just changing their appearance. They also changed what they said and how they said it. This is called code-switching, when we adjust outward markers of an identity (language, gestures, mannerisms, clothing, hairstyle) according to where we are and whom we're with.[8] For instance, you might speak differently around your college-educated coworkers than you do in your low-income neighborhood. You might dress differently around your parents than you do around your closest friends. Code-switching is one of the ways we can weather the strongest of urges to change who we are by compromising. We don't have to permanently give up what makes us *us*. We just have to put on the right face for others until we're back on safe ground.

Everyone code-switches—perhaps people with marginalized identities more so to survive in environments that weren't built with them in mind. Michelle Obama, in her book *Becoming*, spoke of how moving from her largely Black neighborhood on the South Side of Chicago to college at Princeton and Harvard and then to the legal profession taught her several different ways of communicating. "At this point, I thought of myself basically as trilingual," she writes. "I knew the relaxed patois of the South Side and the high-minded diction of the Ivy League, and now on top of that I spoke Lawyer, too."[9]

Code-switching may be an effective strategy, but it's one that many wish didn't have to exist. Tanisha resented that she needed to code-switch to placate her predominantly white clients. "I'm not going against my morality in a sense. But I am going against the authenticity of who I am just to appease and make another group of people comfortable." In a similar way, Shyen could tolerate the stress of code-switching and passing at work only by telling themselves that it was temporary.

Identity Is Fluid

Remember when you were young and you learned about solids, liquids, and gases in your science class? Solids behave in one way, liquids in another, and gases in yet another. Solids are like rocks. Liquids are like water. Gases are like air. Only when we get older do we learn that states of matter are a little more complicated. Some things can be a solid, liquid, and gas at different times. Others can be both a solid and a liquid at the same time. Some solids turn straight to gas or gases straight to solids. And what even is plasma anyway?

We learn about identity in a similar way. We learn the simple (but technically incorrect) information first and then slowly realize the subject is messier than we thought.

What are some of the false ideas that we were taught about identity?

- *Identities have the same meaning to all people who have them.* Ask ten women to define "womanhood," and you'll get ten different answers. Identity labels can be powerful ways to understand ourselves, but the wiggle room within each gives us many ways to define ourselves as we see fit.

- *Identities are always active.* We are all to some degree a blend of privileged and marginalized identities, and which identity winds up being most salient at any given time can depend on the situation. For instance, Inge might walk into a department store and experience white privilege (doting attention from salesclerks and no one tailing her to see if she's stealing) and then in the same afternoon pick her son up from school and experience discrimination due to her queer identity (other parents subtly ignoring her and avoiding offers of playdates). We have so many identities that at any given time we're swapping some out for others, combining two or more, and tinkering with our many selves.

- *Identities stay constant over time.* As people grow and encounter new experiences, their identities change as well. An identity that was once important at one stage in life can become less important at a later one and vice versa. For example, your faith may have been important to you as an adolescent but then become less so in your twenties or thirties.

- *Identities are stable across context and situation.* What happens if you're mixed race but get read as white in some spaces and as Latinx in others? What happens if you're disabled, but on good days you're able to perform most tasks just as well as able-bodied people? We may be tempted to try and reduce our experiences to simple, one-dimensional identities. But life is complicated and, for most of us, not as stable as we'd like. Our identities are likely the same way.

We've all run up against situations where identities important to us come with a cost. Since getting rid of who we are is not always an option (or desirable), we might make the choice to downplay or hide parts of ourselves to get what we need.

Chapter 4

It's Mine
to Sell

We've seen stories about how the identities important to us can clash with our ambitions and desires, but what if they're aligned? What happens when we're given the choice to sell the identities that make us *us*, in exchange for money, power, influence, or respect?

When we're used to our identities being seen as burdens on others, the opportunity to finally be rewarded and not punished for being different can be tantalizing. But such rewards come from people and organizations with their own agendas. While the decision can seem easy at first, those who are offered deals that are too good to be true find that these can start to feel like impossible choices too.

Jovan

Jovan, who uses he/him and also they/them pronouns, has a number of identities and experiences that the world considers disadvantaged: he is Black, queer, trans, and disabled. While he has always been aware of the ways these identities make life harder for him, he is perhaps more aware of others' expectations and assumptions about each of these identities and what they mean. The reason? So he can say the right things to succeed in a world that wasn't built for people like him.

46

From a young age, Jovan learned to play up his various identities from his parents, who had done the same with their own identities. "In public school we have yearly state tests and we have to write an essay. I usually wrote, 'As a Black person . . .' My parents have been doing the same thing. They coached me through it as a kid."

For Jovan, this experience of self-commodification culminated in his college applications. "When I imagine admissions boards, I imagine a table full of white people that don't know anything about Black, brown, queer, or trans experiences but find them super fascinating," Jovan

In March 2019, the FBI revealed that fifty people participated in a massive scam designed to get children from wealthy families into elite universities.[1] This scandal highlights a difference in how the public has historically discussed two ways children can get a leg up in college admissions: financial donations and legacy admissions on the one hand and affirmative action, designed to help underrepresented minority groups, on the other. While both are widely known to influence college admissions, affirmative action tends to be questioned.

"It's so written into the American imagination that these spots (at prestigious institutions) are for white people, and anytime a black student or Latinx student gets in, it's taking a spot away from them," Anthony Jack, an assistant professor of education at Harvard University, told CNN. "That's not what's happening."[2]

explained. "My parents said, 'Just cater to that. Say that you're the only queer person in all of Texas and that that experience is what makes you valuable to whatever school you apply to.'" Jovan followed this advice and told the story that he knew admissions officers wanted:

> When you're applying to college, they want some success story and some tragic backstory. I talked about growing up and being disabled. I talked about how hard it was growing up as a Black person in a predominantly white area. My life was difficult—just not as bad as it could have been. I know elite colleges need Black people, and I just gave them the "trauma porn" story they expected to hear from someone like me. I went out of my way to include stuff about my race. I didn't think it was important, but I thought that other people would think it was important to me, so I just catered to that.

Despite discussing his own selling out so casually, Jovan is extremely intentional regarding when self-commodifying to get what he wants is appropriate. His decision to sell out is based on his critical interpretation of what resource he's aiming for, who it's intended for, and who else is in the room:

> I know there are Black trans people who have way worse lives than I do.[3] If they're in the room, I should save my story for another time and let them take whatever. I'm always making sure I'm not taking space from people who actually need a resource or who have real stories that need to be shared. We all have stories, but some of them are more necessary than others.

In other words, if the resources are earmarked for equality or social justice, they should go to the most marginalized first. Jovan is happy to play the role if no one else seems more deserving.

Jovan's matter-of-fact attitude stems partially from his belief that his actions are not unusual:

> Every single person I know has sold their identities in some way for social or monetary gain. You sell it for scholarships, for jobs. Even if you're trying to get into a fraternity house you have to sell certain aspects of your identity just to fit in. It happens constantly. And sometimes people don't even realize it—it's just emphasizing certain parts of yourself that you know people want or like.

"It kinda sucks, but I've been doing that my whole life," Jovan explained. To him, selling out is a transaction that brings him no particular joy—but nonetheless brings benefits that he may as well take advantage of as he continues through college. "That's the point of diversity boards and scholarships," he concluded, laughing, "so that people can write their tragic backstories for money."

Lam

Lam, who uses they/them pronouns, wanted to become a social worker. As a nonbinary Asian American person in their twenties who had grown up amid discrimination, homelessness, and substance abuse, Lam was fully aware that the frontline workers doing social work often didn't look like the clients they served.[4] To that end, Lam reluctantly made the decision to go to college.

Months into their first year of college, however, Lam was perplexed. People were paying attention to them—a lot of attention. When Lam shared their history around homelessness and substance abuse, people's eyes widened, whether they were students or professors. Students pushed Lam to describe their experiences in the same academic terms they were learning in class. Professors encouraged Lam to identify and even fill in gaps in the academic literature. "Me, contribute research to advance an entire field?" The validation was intoxicating. Maybe, Lam mused, they didn't have to become a social worker after all. Maybe academia would work out.

Newly emboldened, Lam conducted a major research project that examined the experiences of LGBTQ+ homeless people living in a nearby homeless shelter. "This entire world of research and academia and advocacy opened up," they said. "It was the first time in my life where I felt like I could be myself and proud of who I was and that my experience mattered." As the research project continued, however, Lam started feeling strange about their interactions with other academics:

> When I opened up about my experiences I got a lot of affirmation; I got a lot of understanding—it felt very liberating. And at the same time, there was a strange pressure. Other people would say, "You know about this stuff; you've been there. Tell us about your experiences being homeless or with substance abuse or as a minority member."

Lam increasingly noticed how the peers and professors they told about their work seemed more interested in Lam's relationship to the research topic than the research itself. "It was like I was a spokesperson for these communities, for these groups, in a way that I don't think I ever got comfortable with," they explained.

Lam was uncomfortable disclosing personal details to eager strangers but hoped that by doing so these people would care about Lam's research findings more. Lam hesitantly told a few individuals about their own LGBTQ+ identities and about their struggles as a teen. But others didn't react how Lam wanted them to:

People weren't asking about the organizations they should donate to or how to make the problem better or how they could contribute to the research I was doing. It was more about "Let's pat ourselves on the back now."

I mostly felt confused and cheated. I had been told my whole life that there was this adult/professional world that had answers and was open-minded, accepting of challenges, and strived as a whole to create a better, more equal and compassionate world. What I saw and learned while doing that research project seemed to me like the complete opposite of what I had been told.

It made me realize that this adult/professional world that had been lauded to me for so long as the end-all, be-all was just as much BS as the adults, teachers, and students I had been bullied by as a kid. This was earth-shattering to me.

My mental health was affected, my sense of self was affected, and my feelings of self-loathing skyrocketed. I felt caught up in a web and didn't understand how to untangle myself—I hated these institutions I had participated in and at the same time had such a hunger to be validated by them.

Faculty at institutions of higher learning heavily skew toward straight, white, and cisgender.[5] As a result, students who identify as queer and people of color lack role models and mentors, grant money is disproportionately allotted toward the research interests of the privileged, and classrooms struggle with cultural and pedagogical issues around diversity and inclusion.[6]

Lam gave up on academia. They graduated college and used their degree to start working as a drug and alcohol counselor for their local community, as they had initially wanted. This time, they kept their LGBTQ+ identity and their past under wraps with their colleagues.

As a social worker, Lam connected extremely well with their clients and advocated on their behalf to their coworkers. Now they had a new problem: they were so effective that others became suspicious. "I run into a lot of people who question why I'm saying what I'm saying or where I get the information I'm getting," Lam explained. They knew the trade-offs of coming out. Sharing their own identities might help them gain the respect and understanding they needed to be an effective advocate. But their experience in college taught them to be wary of selling their identities, even when the cause seemed justified.

Lam chose to come out, as they always did. They realized after many months that coming out didn't feel like a choice at all. "In my mind at the time, my LGBTQ+ identities were all I had because I consistently had those parts of me honed in on by society. There's so much more of me."

As Lam's career has progressed, they've also started trying to be kinder to themself and make new resolutions, such as finding community among people with shared identities so that they can be themself around others with a shared language. "I crave connection," they said. "But I feel safer making connections within my own communities."

Finding a validating place to be themself helps Lam resist the pull to performatively share their identities. "That need to reveal my identity or come out to people just to support what I'm saying isn't something that I should do unless I feel like it's for *me*. Engaging in that kind of behavior for other people is a damaging part of that internalized self-hatred that I took on." Lam to has realized that the problem isn't always internal. "Sometimes my intention when I speak out is not from the desire to sell out, but the way people respond to me elicits a feeling like I'm a sellout," they explained. "If more people understood that my identities shouldn't be seen as a commodity, these interactions would feel better."

Even if they aren't always sure whether they're selling out, Lam has become more comfortable with the ambiguity. "Sometimes I occupy a space that can feel nice and terrible. Sometimes I'm able to speak out about a lot of things, and it sometimes crosses into the territory where I'm not sure if I'm doing it for myself or for other people." Lam, however, is working on it. "There's a lot of strength just in being myself," they said.

Markwayne

Markwayne Mullin, who uses he/him pronouns, has been a Republican congressman for Oklahoma's second Congressional District since 2013 and is an enrolled member of the Cherokee Nation. He is one of only four Native Americans in the 116th Congress and proudly touts his Cherokee heritage on his website and promotional materials, where he claims that he "brings a firsthand knowledge of Native American issues to Washington, D.C."[7] When he was elected to congress, he tearfully accepted a ceremonial blanket from Cherokee Nation Chief Bill John Baker.[8]

Yet Markwayne's Cherokee citizenship was far from visible when he first ran for Congress. In fact, his Native American identity was made public only later that year, when Chief Bill John Baker—the same one who would gift him a ceremonial blanket the following year—refused to endorse him, instead donating $2,500 to his Democratic opponent.[9] An AP article reported that, despite his criticisms of federal funding as a "horrible waste of tax dollars," Markwayne had benefited from his tribe's Indian preference policy to receive over $350,000 in federal stimulus money.[10]

Since being elected, Markwayne has continued to take stances that outrage his Cherokee constituents. In 2013, he toed the Tea Party line and repeatedly voted against the Violence Against Women Act, a bill that would have closed a loophole allowing violence against Native women to go unprosecuted.[11] In 2017, he advocated for privatizing tribal lands to open them up for deregulated drilling for oil, gas, and coal.[12] And in 2018, he referred to the Trail of Tears, the forced migration of over sixteen thousand Cherokee to Oklahoma that left thousands dead, as a "voluntary walk" during an interview on Fox News.[13]

Many Native critics have noted both Markwayne's readiness to capitalize on his Cherokee identity and his track record of consistently acting against Native interests. Twila Barnes, a Cherokee writer, asserts that this behavior invalidates Markwayne's Cherokee identity and that he has forgotten who he is:

> For most of us, "Cherokee first" means we are Cherokee first, and all other things, like being members of a US political party, come after that. For Markwayne Mullin, it seems "Cherokee first" only means he gets to cut to the front of the line for a job that has Indian preference.[14]

Native writer Louis Fowler shares this critique, arguing that Native identity has always been about cultural pride and standing up for one's community, and that Markwayne's failure to protect Native interests makes him a sellout:

> When you look at Oklahoma's long history of Indian sellouts, those that sold off their heritage to feast on the table-scraps from the higher-ups, Mullin is just another damned soul ready to throw on the pyre.

... Mullin is ... a Native sellout of the highest order that uses his heritage as a nice line in his biography, but then immediately scrubs it when he's afraid it might lose him some good Republican voters.[15]

Dr. Karen Biestman, director of the Native American Cultural Center and lecturer in law and Native American studies at Stanford University, argues that the cultural commodification of Native and indigenous identities has been spurred by the simultaneous disenchantment with organized religion and explosion of interest in ancient and indigenous spiritual practices: drumming groups, goddess worship, and earth-based religions. In the process, Native American culture has been reclaimed and romanticized. Biestman elaborated, "People who participate in commodification of this kind are morally justified in their minds due to a fiction of reverence for the culture."[16]

As a result of this idealization, Indian-inspired goods and services are a huge industry. Executives shell out $10,000 a week apiece to attend Native-inspired "warriors retreats." The New Age industry has exploded with stores selling incense, sage, and healing crystals. Many Native folks find this commercialized and watered-down version of Native practices to be problematic. The Lakota tribe, for instance, has issued a declaration of war against New Ageism.[17]

Reflection

At its heart, Lam's story is about *compassion* and *honesty*. They realized that, despite being uncomfortable with being seen only as a compilation of marginalized identities, they would often willingly paint themselves into that corner. They eventually recognized that their urge to self-commodify stemmed from a lack of community, connection, and validation in their life. Rather than shame themself for wanting to sell their identity for approval, they sought to meet their needs through healthier means.

Jovan and Markwayne's stories are both fundamentally about *accountability*. While we weren't able to find Markwayne's own words about how he holds himself accountable to his constituents, numerous articles by Cherokee writers accuse him of selling out: lacking accountability to the Cherokee community while championing his Cherokee identity when it benefits him. Jovan, despite being one of the rare few who willingly identified as a sellout, had a robust internal code to keep himself accountable to his belief system. This code allowed him to sell out whenever the opportunity presented itself without concern that he was compromising anything sacred.

Culture: For Sale

American culture has long mysticized the unknown "other." Whether the uncharted frontier of manifest destiny (which was very much inhabited and charted, just not by white people) or the ancient traditions of the east (which were just as dubious as the ancient traditions of the west), what is unfamiliar is in equal parts terrifying and alluring.

Being seen as other means that the physical and social world often isn't built for you. Buildings aren't accessible to people in wheelchairs. Automatic sinks don't turn on for people with darker skin. Workplaces recognize only Christian holidays. Survey options don't include all genders.

However, the same individualist societies that perpetuate these inequalities can also offer a back door to personal gain: selling an othered identity or experience for the appeal of an exotic identity.[18] The impossible choices related to this selling can carry costs that reach beyond individual discomfort. By using their identities to self-commodify, members of marginalized and minority groups can inadvertently give power to the corporate and social actors looking to benefit off of difference. Markwayne's story and the backlash of other Cherokee who felt harmed by his words and actions illustrate this well.

Historically, Native Americans have been subject to both some of the most egregious violence and some of the most romanticized interest in the United States. Some Native American populations declined by 90 percent or more within a century of European contact, a calamity that has been described as "the greatest demographic disaster ever."[19] Centuries of exploitation and violence have left their mark: 26.2 percent of Native Americans today are in poverty, compared to 14 percent of the total US population.[20]

These economic conditions serve as the backdrop for contentious discussions involving self-commodification and selling out, especially in struggling communities that have no other option. For example, is it commodification if a small urban Native community sells Native American trinkets and dream catchers to pay the rent or if a tribe strapped for cash sells permission to a football team to use their name? According to many Cherokee critics, Markwayne's comfortable Congressman income is no excuse for his self-commodification. Native American history is full of cases where Natives had to sell out to survive; Markwayne, it appears, is not one of those cases.

Benevolent Prejudices

Members of marginalized or minority groups often have the uncomfortable experience of realizing that people in their lives view them through the lens of stereotypes. Oftentimes, these stereotypes cast marginalized or minority groups as less competent, less desirable, less intelligent, or even less human than others. Other times, these stereotypes can take the form of *benevolent prejudices*. Benevolent prejudices or stereotypes are beliefs about a group that may superficially appear positive but are nevertheless harmful. For example, the belief that gay men are more fun, Black people are better at dancing, and women are more compassionate are all benevolent prejudices.[21]

For example, Inge's colleague Jana, a Black Caribbean woman, was often asked to start parties. "The composition of my friends was majority white," she explained. "If there was any dancing involved, they'd ask me as the resident Black person to dance to get the party started. I like dancing so I'd do it." Then Jana realized that her friends were not comfortable starting the party themselves. What first appeared to be a friendly suggestion ("You like to dance; here's an opportunity!") turned sinister in the light of her new knowledge that people saw her first and foremost as the party-starter—which almost certainly had to do with her racial background. "It was as if they were saying, 'Jana, dance so *we* can feel comfortable,'" she explained. Suddenly, she was faced with an uncomfortable choice: have fun and dance, knowing she was being used, or refuse to participate in benevolent racism and sacrifice some of her own fun too? "I didn't like to have voyeurs while dancing. Once I caught on, I stopped dancing until I felt comfortable. Sometimes that meant I never danced."

Like Jana, members of marginalized and minority groups are often aware of what sells, what stories and behaviors evoke interest, curiosity, sympathy, and wonder from others. Jovan was taught by his parents that selling his story—with some slight embellishments—could fast-track his access to resources such as scholarships. Lam gained academic approval through sharing stories about their upbringing. However, the cost of these selling-out opportunities is often less clear. Sometimes these costs are borne by the individual doing the selling out—for example, Jana would have to struggle through knowing that she was being used for her energy and Blackness. Other times, however, the costs of selling out are borne by the community.

Staying You

Self-commodification has its benefits, but its costs can come in the form of losing touch with what makes you *you*. Lam experienced this and realized that they were increasingly playing a caricature of themselves by talking only about the experiences that others wanted to hear. Coming to terms with the exploitative nature of their relationship with academia and academics prompted their desire to leave, but even in their new job the urge to self-commodify was strong. Part of their healing process involves finding community spaces where they can meet others like them and engage authentically without the voyeuristic eyes of outsiders. Their goal is to reach a place of comfort where they no longer act on the urge to play a character in front of others.

Jovan, on the other hand, hasn't had much trouble staying himself, despite his constant self-commodification. Rather than see what he does as a reflection on himself, he reframes it as a conscious strategy he uses in specific scenarios. Years of experience have given Jovan a sense of ease with putting on various masks in different situations to get what he wants. For him, it's okay to flex or even exaggerate parts of his identity or story in the moment because he knows that his underlying self isn't at risk. Jovan's secret: "Know my boundaries. Some people want to hear every single gory detail about your life. Remember that not everyone deserves to hear everything about yourself."

Some people see selling ones' identities as a way to get a foot in the door when one is otherwise disadvantaged; others see it as a manipulation that reflects poorly on one's community. Where is the line when it comes to selling identity? When is it a survival strategy or a way to balance the impact of historical discrimination, and when is it a betrayal to one's community? Although the answers aren't always clear, several factors are worth considering:

- Is one's original culture or self being respected and authentically portrayed, or is it being misrepresented for the sake of an outside audience or consumer? Authentic portrayals have the potential to educate, whereas misrepresentations can spread misinformation and reinforce stereotypes.

- Are the people most in need benefiting from the commodification, versus those who already have a host of other options or resources? Some self-commodification may benefit only the business owners, entrepreneurs, or others who are capitalizing on their own cultural history, while others who share the same identities receive no benefit but all the disadvantages. For instance, the Florida Seminole tribes benefit financially from Florida State's use of the Seminole name, but the Oklahoma Seminole tribes—a much larger group—receive no benefit from the commodification of the Seminole brand, yet are still impacted by the resulting perpetuation of false stereotypes (Florida State game days still include fan rituals such as "war-chanting" and "tomahawk-chopping").[22]

- Who's making the decisions about whether to commodify and about how the person or community is being portrayed, and who gets to weigh in? Ideally, the people most impacted by the commodification and those with true cultural expertise are also the primary decision-makers.

· Chapter 5 ·

The Sellout Crisis

Sometimes a situation offers us time to ponder our choices and think carefully about next steps. Other times a spotlight shines suddenly on us and we're forced to pick between two things we care deeply about. These situations are a special brand of impossible choice that we call a *sellout crisis*. Without the time to reframe, rationalize, or justify, we're put in a situation where we have to rely on our gut to make the right choice.

Sellout crises happen all the time. When a person you care about makes an offensive comment and you have a few seconds to decide whether to confront it or let it go, that's a potential sellout crisis. When a person you've just met makes an incorrect assumption about one of your identities that, if left uncorrected, could put you at a significant advantage, that's a potential sellout crisis as well. What do you do when doing the right thing or standing up for your beliefs entails a loss and you have no time to think? When does selling out happen not as a premeditated choice but as a deer-in-headlights response?

Beth

Beth, who uses she/her pronouns, pulled her blanket a little more closely around her shoulders, trying to trap as much warmth as possible. It was February and her house had no heat. She had called numerous repair companies, but because of the problematic way the heater had been installed, it was going to be very hard to fix. Two companies had already come out and been unable to fix the heater, several had refused to come out altogether based on the installation, still others were booked until spring, and Beth was getting desperate.

When the repairman from the third company showed up, Beth had been without heat for weeks, and she was determined to find a way to resolve the situation this time. Maybe she could play up a damsel-in-distress role: "Please help me, I'm so cold!"

Then she noticed that the repairman was wearing a yarmulke. Beth herself was Jewish—kind of. Born to a Jewish mother and Catholic father, Beth had been raised interfaith, having a bat mitzvah ceremony but also regularly celebrating Christmas. Currently she identified as agnostic, with Judaism holding more of a cultural than religious place in her life. But Beth's experience with Jewish communities told her that Jews who wore yarmulkes often had a special affinity for other Jews, and she decided to milk that for all it was worth.

"I'm Jewish," she told the repairman.

Her statement got his attention. He began asking her questions, seemingly to test whether she was legitimately Jewish: What was her Jewish name? What Jewish rituals had she participated in? Beth knew enough to answer his questions convincingly. Although none of her answers were exactly lies, she was acutely aware that she had avoided mentioning her Catholic father, and that felt like a betrayal.

The repairman, for his part, warmed up to Beth. He stopped quizzing her and started confiding in her. The state of Jews in America had reached a crisis point, he lamented: "They're all marrying off to non-Jews!" Beth felt an uncomfortable twinge: she herself was the product of such a union. But she nodded in agreement.

The repairman went on to speak for almost thirty minutes regarding what he perceived as the victimization and inherent superiority of the Jewish people. Beth found many of his comments objectionable or even appalling but she said nothing:

> In any other capacity in my life, I think I would have stopped this person and said, "What you're saying I don't agree with; this is really offensive to me. Quite honestly you're giving a bad name to Jews by even speaking this way." I was super conscious in the moment of what I was doing. But I was really, really hoping that I could endear this person to me.

Beth felt ashamed of her own behavior; she felt she had sold out:

> I was acting out of alignment with my own authenticity, but I just wanted to get my heat fixed. It happened to be during a crazy cold wave. It was legit cold. It was like fifty degrees in my house and I was feeling desperate. I'm incredibly close to my father. I have attended Mass with him on many occasions in my life. And so it did feel like I was erasing him and making him invisible in that moment. It didn't feel good. It felt shameful and it also felt like it was a lie. I really don't identify strongly with Jewish tradition or Jewish culture or Jewish life. So I absolutely claimed a higher level of identity salience than feels authentic to me.

Looking back on her experience, Beth doesn't feel proud of her choices, but she also acknowledged that the situation escalated rapidly from what she had at first expected:

> I don't think I did anything that wrong, but I definitely elevated a part of my identity for personal gain. It's

Although people commonly presume that children from interfaith marriages will be raised in one faith or the other, those who were raised or identify as mixed faith represent a significant cohort. According to the NPR podcast *Code Switch*, people with mixed identity backgrounds commonly feel like imposters or fakes but are less clear which identity they're faking: both (or all) identities are real and yet incomplete on their own. Observers often project one identity or another onto a mixed-identity person according to what's most salient to them.[1]

maybe not the most moral choice I've ever made, but I don't think it was that bad. It became extra awkward when it wasn't just me trying to be like, "What up? We're both Jews. Like cool." It was that he ended up saying all these things about Jews and gentiles that were really misaligned with how I feel. And then I was stuck in this role that I put myself in by trying to align with him.

In the end, Beth's interaction with the repairman won him over and he advocated on her behalf with his manager that they should try to fix the heater. Unfortunately, the manager said no. Her heat still isn't fixed.

Audre

Audre Lorde, a Black lesbian, acclaimed writer, womanist, and civil rights activist who used she/her pronouns, described a sellout crisis experience in her essay "Is Your Hair Still Political?" About to board a plane for a Caribbean vacation, Audre was stopped by an immigration officer who refused to let her board because her hair, which was in locks, was deemed illegal. Audre protested, taken completely aback by what seemed like an arbitrary law and argued to no avail with the officer—who was herself a Black woman. Finally, a supervisor appeared—a Black man. "Are you a Rasta?" he asked.

> He didn't ask me if I was a murderer. He didn't ask me if I was a drug dealer, or a racist, or if I was a member of the Ku Klux Klan. Instead, he asked me if I was a follower of the Rastafarian religion.
>
> Some see locks and they see revolution. Because Rastafarians smoke marijuana as a religious rite, some see locks and automatically see drug peddlers. But the people who are pushing drugs throughout the Caribbean do not wear locks; they wear three-piece suits, carry attaché cases and diplomatic pouches, and usually have no trouble at all passing through Immigration.
>
> I stared at this earnest young Black man for a moment. Suddenly my hair became very political. Waves of horror washed over me. How many forms of religious persecution are we now going to visit upon each other as Black people in the name of our public safety?[2]

Audre felt angry and torn that she had been profiled and that those doing the profiling were Black like herself. She wanted to point out the hypocrisy and prejudice in the question she was asked. She wanted to say, "What does it matter if I'm a Rasta or not?"

> But I saw our bags sitting out in the sun, and the pilot walking slowly back to his plane. Deep in my heart I thought—*it is always the same question: where do we begin to take a stand?* But I turned away.

Black people with locks are often the target of discrimination based on the incorrect assumption that locks are dirty or unkempt. In 2010, a woman named Chastity Jones had her job offer rescinded when she declined to cut her locks off for the job. In 2016, the Eleventh Federal Court ruled that it is legal for an employer to ban dreadlocks during the hiring process.[3]

"No, I'm not a Rastafarian," I said. And true, I am not. But deep inside of me I felt I was being asked to deny some piece of myself, and I felt a solidarity with my Rastafarian brothers and sisters that I had never been conscious of before.[4]

In one moment, a vacation with a friend had turned into a confrontation with persecution, profiling, and discrimination. Audre was faced with a sellout crisis, but the cause felt far larger than herself. If she had stood her ground, what could she have done? How could she live her values, fight for the right cause, and win? With her denial, Audre was allowed to board the plane and start her vacation. But the choice left a bitter taste in her mouth. "The sun was still shining," she recalled, "but somehow the day seemed less bright."[5]

Ben

Ben, an older white man who uses he/him pronouns, was looking forward to this conversation. He had just been recommended by the president of an up-and-coming corporation to serve on its board, a rare opportunity that promised to be both professionally gratifying and financially lucrative. The company specialized in customized automation for industries around the world. To be invited to the board of such a corporation was a great honor.

Yet Ben started having misgivings not long into the conversation with the company president. As excited as the man seemed about his technology, he hadn't said a word about how he was going to manage the disruptions it would cause. "As we were talking, it became very clear to me that he had no concern about laying off workers," Ben told us. "It was just instrumentally dealing with the device and how much money he could get from the customers. It pushed my buttons." As the conversation went on, Ben realized that this man's lack of care about the impacts of his technology on workers might be a deal breaker. "I didn't want to be associated with anything that would take away people's jobs," Ben explained, "and yet I was tempted by the offer, which included substantial stock options."

Then the moment came: "What do you say?" the company president asked. In the heat of the moment, Ben's gut feeling told him this was bad news, and he made a choice on the spot. "I felt that it was over the line for me morally in terms of my values," he explained. Ben said no. He wouldn't join the board.

As a result of automation, up to 375 million people worldwide, or 14 percent of all workers, will need to change occupations and learn new skills by 2030 to stay employed, according to a 2018 report from the McKinsey Global Institute. A significant number of these workers will likely be left behind, unable to keep up with the rapidly changing demands to stay employable.[6]

"But then something sort of funny happened," Ben continued.

> The president of the company said, "Well, why wouldn't you?" And when I explained my reservations, he became holier-than-thou, saying that he would never do this, I misunderstood him, and so forth. He assured me he shared my concerns and would not be doing the things I objected to.
>
> Did I really believe it? I wasn't sure. Automation is designed to take away human tasks, after all, yet all it took was that little nudge to get me to set aside my conscience. He made it easy for me to reverse and accept, so I did.

The conversation ended and both men got up to leave. Ben was still thinking about his decision. "I was wondering if I'd let myself off the hook too easily because they weren't the world's greatest social company. It wasn't that clear-cut."

Ben's experience on the board was fulfilling and ultimately quite lucrative. Despite this positive experience, Ben has never forgotten that earlier conversation. Did he make the right choice? Years later, he still isn't sure. "I could feel good that I had stuck with my principles or I could have said, 'He gave me an easy excuse to not be so firm about my principles and compromise them.' To this day, I don't know which view is the right one. I choose to say I stuck to my principles. But it may have been a little bit of both." Part of his insecurity stems from the fact that Ben has seen his friends rationalize away real moral problems and is wary of doing so himself. "A lot of my friends rationalize. When they're faced with a moral crisis, they make it okay, but it really isn't okay, I wondered how much of that I had done that day."

Ben is glad that he said yes, even though he's still unsure about whether he compromised his values. "I think the world is no worse off for it," he concluded. "I'm a lot better off for it. So I think I made the right decision. Was I totally pure in doing so? I doubt it."

Reflection

Sellout crises are perhaps the most universal of the experiences we share in this book. Nearly everyone has been in an awkward, uncomfortable, or tense situation that demanded a quick response. Beth and Audre grappled with honesty and accountability in the face of benign situations that rapidly changed, forcing them into split-second decisions that felt out of line with their values. Beth struggled to accurately represent herself to the repairman amid a quickly devolving conversation. Audre held her tongue rather than waylay her plans, calling into question her personal responsibility for defending other Black communities.

Oftentimes we can feel tempted to judge ourselves for choices we made in the moment. We think, "If only I'd had time to think about that, I would have done something differently!" Yet sellout crises happen in a split second; that's practically their definition. Given this, we were struck by the openness with which Ben reflected on his decision after the fact. Ben's honesty combined with self-compassion allowed him to ponder if he had rationalized his decision and approach it from a space of curiosity rather than shame.

Sellout Crises Happen Every Day

When we think of compromising situations, we might think of a high-stakes, dramatic moment like those we see in pop culture. The hero must choose between saving the world and saving a romantic interest. The friend-turned-traitor is paid off by the enemy and learns just how much one's loyalty is worth. Maybe this is one reason why we struggle so much with making these choices in real life: oftentimes, no one can see our sellout crisis but ourselves. The dramatic moment passes in an instant, leaving us with only the beeping of our moral smoke detector as we work to make peace with our choices. One way or another, we find a way to deal with the beeping.

Beth, Audre, and Ben were all left in this exact situation. Beth sat shivering in her unheated home. Audre's vacation had a long shadow cast over it. Ben was left with a nagging feeling in the back of his mind. What's interesting about such experiences is that they happen so frequently that we don't fully metabolize them. In a world where our values are invisible and society moves fast, compromises are not only ubiquitous but practically ignored.

Because so many of our "microcrises" are ignored, relying on our moral smoke detector and knowing when a compromise was genuinely concerning can be difficult. Perhaps the answer is that the sellout crises we think about are the ones that matter. We think about sellout crises in our lives when they involve new or unfamiliar ideas, like when Beth was pulled into a "Jewish-enough" role-playing session. We think about sellout crises when they reveal truths about ourselves and the world, like when Audre felt a jolt of solidarity with Black Rastafarians. And finally, we think about sellout crises when they're awkward, like when Ben's refusal to join the board was met with accusations that he was being judgmental.

The truth is, how we feel when we're in the middle of a sellout crisis almost doesn't matter. Good luck formulating a counterargument, clarifying a point, or correcting a mistake in the two to three seconds you have. What matters most is how we look back on and interpret what happened. We say "interpret" and not "remember" to recognize that as humans, our memories of individual moments aren't as spot-on as we think they are.[7] Try it yourself: exactly how were you feeling when you started eating breakfast yesterday? Chances are, you won't remember.

Sellout crises happen every day, yet we hardly pay attention to them. In many ways this is convenient—it ensures that we minimize conflict when unnecessary. But minimizing conflict isn't always good. When the microcrisis becomes a full-blown crisis, knowing what to do is important.

· Chapter 6 ·

The Greater Good

Typically, we think of selling out as a choice that's made to access something desirable, such as money or power, that would otherwise be out of reach. But as we have witnessed in the previous chapters, people can sell out when they realize that they have too much to lose. Like many others, the people you will meet in this chapter were faced with impossible choices. Unlike them, however, these individuals were faced with pressure to compromise not their identities but primarily their beliefs and values.

For many of us, our values are sacred. They shape our morals, influence our personal and professional goals, and help give our lives direction when we don't know what to do. These stories are about people who faced a moment of reckoning when their values were put up against something they wanted or needed and what happened when they felt compelled to choose the greater good.

Mahogany

"There's no such thing as culture in psychology."

Mahogany, who uses she/her pronouns, blinked and stared at her professor, not sure if he was joking or not. He wasn't. The older white man was genuinely insisting that the study of psychology had no room for talk of *culture*—the rich backgrounds, histories, beliefs, and values that make us who we are.

Mahogany, a Black Christian woman who had started out working in the corporate world and then had gone back to school to change careers, was in the final class needed for her doctorate in psychology. The class on psychodynamic theory was taught by the chair of the department, and she had to pass it to get her degree.

But her professor was talking nonsense, and Mahogany wasn't having it. She was raised by her parents to be proud of her Blackness and the richness of nonwhite histories, and the very reason she had pursued a psychology doctorate in the first place was because she had seen herself and her culture represented in contemporary psychological work. Who was this man to insult and erase a history that meant so much to her?

I said to him, "All the second- and third-wave Chicano scholars and black scholars and Asian scholars and womanist scholars—they're not in your syllabus. So that's how you can get to 'there's no culture.' You just literally stopped in the '60s when there was an explosion. What happened from the '60s to the present is how I can survive and be in this field. And you're obliterating it."

Despite what Mahogany asserted, her professor continued to insist on his characterization of psychology. As the semester progressed, tensions continued to rise between the two as they disagreed over the same sets of issues. Mahogany felt that she had both an academic and a deeply personal stake in challenging her professor: she could not embrace the all-white, pre-1960s curriculum in which people like her were conspicuously absent and regurgitate these partial histories for a grade.

At the end of the semester, her resistance had consequences. The professor refused to give her credit for the course, claiming that Mahogany didn't have what it takes to engage in psychodynamic work.

Mahogany was stuck in limbo. To graduate her doctoral program, she had no choice but to take the same course again with the same professor. It was unlikely that the second time around he would take any more kindly to her many critiques of his class. If anything, he would be more suspicious of her and apply a higher standard to her than to his other students. Mahogany was faced with a dilemma: if she questioned her professor again, or even offered a neutral response to his teachings, she risked failing the course and thus being unable to graduate and realize her dream of becoming a psychologist. However, to go along with teachings that she felt were toxic in their ignorance of cultural context felt traitorous to her values.

Was she really up for spending months telling the professor what he wanted to hear? To say, write, and argue points that she rightly believed were more than fifty years outdated and to suppress the wealth of psychodynamic ideas that had pulled her into the field to begin with?

Conflicted, Mahogany looked at a photo of her family, "This is what's gonna get me through," she decided, "because I can't forsake $150,000 [in tuition] and everything I'm going after and my whole dream of being an African American therapist because of this class. My dream is bigger, and one person can't get in the way."

Mahogany took the class again. Her strategy: bow down to the professor, give him only positive feedback, and repeat his beliefs back to him verbatim. "I had this 'Mo-tean' stance," she said, referencing antebellum slaves who served white slaveowners drinks while asking, "Mo' tea, Massa?" When she got the urge to challenge the professor's ideas,

Starting in the 1960s, a wave of new voices and perspectives diversified the field of psychology, resulting in today's wide acceptance among contemporary psychodynamic/psychoanalytic scholars of the role of culture within the field.[1] For one of many examples, see "The Role of Culture in Psychodynamic Psychotherapy: Parallel Process Resulting in Cultural Similarities between Patient and Therapist."[2]

she instead held her tongue. The weeks passed, and after what felt like an eternity, Mahogany completed her final class.

She went on to earn her degree, graduate, and land her first choice of internship. She doesn't regret the choice she made. "I realized that the system was toxic," she said, "and that there are different ways to fight." What she had done to get through the class fit with her values, she decided, because it was a strategic choice in the service of the greater good. Her dream was to continue pushing the field in the direction that her professor was willfully ignorant of, and the impact of her success far outweighed the guilt of compromising her beliefs.

Mahogany noted with a certain degree of satisfaction that she might be getting the last laugh after everything that happened. "The arc of justice is long: the psychology program I was in wants to diversify, and he's an inflexible old white man." There was a good chance that the students after her would never have to make the same decision that she did.

Diana

Diana, who uses she/her pronouns, knew her first job after college would expose her to environments different from the liberal bubble she had left, but she didn't expect them to be *this* different.

In her new role with a company that created environmentally minded products for the ranching industry, the Colombian American queer woman found herself at her first big ranchers conference within weeks of starting her job. In her head, she knew that the industry her company was partnering with was, in her words, "Ninety percent white and 90 percent male, with an average age of fifty-eight." While she had prepared for the demographic change, she soon realized that she hadn't prepared enough for the culture change.

Microaggressions, according to social scientists, are the collective everyday slights motivated by isms and phobias (racism, sexism, ableism, heterosexism, and others) that people from marginalized and minority groups face every day.[3] A poor student may be asked why he can't afford the same expensive drinks as his classmates at a bar. An Iranian American woman may be asked to "speak American" as she calls a family member on the phone. Microaggressions are almost never intentional but more a result of unconscious bias and the assumptions that individuals grow up with. But for marginalized and minority groups, each microaggression can feel like a blow. Day by day, month by month, they wear a person down—an invisible burden that others simply do not see.

On her first day there, a conference-goer learned about Diana's Colombian American background and immediately asked her if she knew any drug traffickers. Another asked if Diana was a "booth babe" (an attractive model hired to make sales at trade shows, often with no knowledge about the product). A third man learned about Diana's college education and immediately remarked, "You got in only because you're a minority." Nobody spoke up in her defense. The casual racist, sexist, and homophobic microaggressions she received that day at the conference were a blunt reminder of where she was.

In college she had learned that the right way to fight microaggressions was to confront them whenever they occurred, whether or not she herself was insulted by the statements. "If you are part of the community, you are an ally to the community," she explained. "If something is said that is problematic, you say something. You don't allow something harmful to your community to go uncontested or else you are not a good member of this community."

But at her next conference, Diana found this commitment to speaking up against prejudice tested. When she overheard a conference attendee speak about transgender people as "creepy" and "disgusting," she felt a powerful urge to confront the man making the comment. However, this person was one of her company's clients, and Diana was at the conference as a representative of her company. So she held her tongue.

How did Diana square her loyalty to her community against her job requirements? "Initially I felt that I was becoming less true to my community," she admitted. "I realized that I couldn't be authentic at work because if I was, I wouldn't be able to do my job. I'm a product manager. I'm supposed to build empathy and connect with these people." That meant connecting with people who held drastically different political views than hers, a tough feat for the outspoken young professional.

If the job had been an office job, she might have left rather than compromise her values. But her company's environmental mission in the Midwest was what had brought Diana there in the first place. Would she leave it behind in the name of her morality?[4]

She decided to stay.

"If this was a job that wasn't social impact minded, if it didn't have an environmental mission, it'd be totally different," she shared with us. "If I was just making sales or making money, then I'd be judging myself still."

> I think of it as an optimization equation. Instead of just thinking if I'm doing the most good for my community, I'm also asking, "Am I making sure that I'm doing the most good for reversing climate change?" If I tap out of doing my role here and choose not to work with Midwestern, Trump-supporting people, if I decide to draw the line there, then environmentally there are consequences. Selling out might suck in the immediate and make me feel like I'm not supporting my community, but as an intersectional eco-feminist I think someone has to go to Middle America. We'd get kicked out really fast if we showed up in our Burning Man gear. That's the balance of things.

Diana was willing to make compromises to continue having an environmental impact, but that didn't mean she would abandon her values entirely. To hold on to her sense of loyalty with the LGBTQ+ community, she started becoming closer to the clients with whom she had developed strong working relationships. As they became not only colleagues but also friends, Diana slowly started sharing more about herself and her identities. "At that point you kind of have to be open-minded with each other," she explained. "It's really rewarding to hit that place."

Yet Diana increasingly looked outside the workplace for validation, joining a cooperative living community and engaging in advocacy work that affirmed her values. These experiences gave Diana a strengthened identification with her community and resulted in something surprising: the more secure she became with her values, the less she worried about selling them out. "You have to feel so much a part of that community that you don't think a single interaction with a third party can bring into question your sense of belonging," she explained. Work, to Diana, was far from the only place she could affirm her values—and she liked it that way.

Reflection

Mahogany and Diana were both able to make *nuanced* and strategic choices when presented with obstacles to their goals. Mahogany's strategy was to qualify her compromise: she bowed down to her closed-minded professor yet was adamant that her acquiescence would last only until she passed the class and not a minute longer. Diana's strategy was to make up for her workplace compromise by creating little wins at work with the clients she trusted. By doing so, she could adapt her compromise to hold on to her value of authenticity and keep her job.

Diana's experience of adapting her compromise is also one of *growth*. She was able to use her discomfort with compromising at work to think deeply about her values. She learned that her desire to speak up at all costs had stemmed partially from being insecure about her loyalty. By participating more in the LGBTQ+ community, Diana was able to strengthen her values, move away from seeing her workplace as the end-all, be-all; and feel more secure, empowered, and self-aware.

Weighing the Options

Mahogany had failed her last class after sticking up for her beliefs. Diana had silently endured a day full of ignorant and bigoted comments. Both women were profoundly uncomfortable as they considered their decision to compromise their values to get what they needed.

If they compromised, every second that Mahogany acted subserviently to her professor and every conversation in which Diana had to fake a smile would be an instance of actively selling out their values. To get through these situations, both women would have to ignore the blaring of their moral smoke detectors. Why would anyone choose to do that?

Unlike in a sellout crisis situation, Mahogany and Diana had time to weigh the pros and cons of their options. Mahogany weighed her pride, her personal relationship to the field of psychology, and her principles as an academic against the money she had invested in her degree and her future career as a psychologist. She couldn't pursue alternatives since her professor wasn't going to budge, and no other classes were available she could take to replace this one. Diana weighed her sense of community and feelings of authenticity against a job that gave her meaning and allowed her to create environmental impact. Diana had more options than Mahogany. She could leave her job, find a creative work-around, or look into options outside of work.

Mahogany's choice was relatively straightforward: her career was worth more than a few months of her pride and outspokenness. When she lined everything up, the scale clearly tipped in one direction.

Diana's choice was more complex. She chose to keep everything—her community, her authenticity, a job with meaning, and social impact—and was willing to shuffle around aspects of her life to do so. At work, she found new ways of reframing her role and engaging in small acts of authenticity that allowed her to survive in a hostile space. And outside of work, she developed new communities to nurture those parts of her that work simply couldn't. Diana was able to mix and match the items on her scale until everything balanced out.

When we find ourselves in situations like the ones Mahogany and Diana went through, we're often forced to make the quintessential impossible choice between two things we're unwilling to give up. Authenticity or career? Loyalty or impact? Mahogany's and Diana's stories illustrate just two of the many different answers to the impossible choice: play the game of short-term compromise and rearrange your life to downsize the choice from impossible to manageable.

Chapter 7

Dancing with Complicity

When we make impossible choices, we frequently must consider whether the costs of compromise are bearable. Sometimes we hide identities important to us or even give them up entirely. Sometimes we compromise our own authenticity or other values that we hold dear. And sometimes our decisions have impacts that are bigger than ourselves.

In this chapter, we explore the stories of people who realized that they were participating in harmful systems and had to make a choice: leave and forfeit everything, or sell out and reconcile their complacency with harm. This choice is never easy, and as you'll see in the next few stories, there's no one right answer.

Abby

The owner of the company Abby worked for was a charming man—all smiles and fast words, as if he was constantly putting on a show to enrapture those around him. Abby, a young professional with a Southern drawl who uses she/her pronouns, was enraptured.

Abby's office manager job was meant to be only a short-term position after college, but she couldn't have predicted how much she would enjoy the praise from her boss, the company owner. He always had a kind word to say about her work and compliments for her in meetings. Abby soaked it all up: "I was very taken with the charisma. I was very subservient, overly appreciative, and eager to please and not at all aware that something could be under the surface."

Along with the praise came something she didn't expect: raises, bonuses, and promotions. The money was an incredible motivator, a validation of her talents and a reward for what she saw as good work. She felt like the heroine of a movie in a success montage; money kept rolling in, and it looked as if she wouldn't be running out of steam anytime soon. It was almost too good to be true.

Turns out, it was. She started hearing whispers of rumors from two of her colleagues, both accountants who crunched the numbers. What they shared almost certainly violated their nondisclosure agreements, but they had reached their breaking point. They had to tell someone, so they told Abby the truth: the owner of the company was embezzling funds. A second set of books had the true numbers on them that no one but the owner and his accountants, bound by their NDAs, could see.

Just how widespread is corporate corruption? The Corruption Perceptions Index, which ranks 180 countries and territories by their perceived levels of public-sector corruption according to industry experts, uses a scale of 0 to 100, in which 0 is highly corrupt and 100 is very clean. Over two-thirds of countries scored below 50 on the most recent CPI (2018). The United States earned a score of 71, which places it just above the United Arab Emirates and Uruguay: better than the rather alarming global average score of 43 but far from something to be proud of.[1]

Abby had suspected this for a while. Why else had her rise to the top been so sharp? "I began to realize that I was being bought," Abby said. "I was good at what I did, but the money was about buying a confidante, buying my silence in an attempt to make me complicit." The thought filled her with anger and indignation, and she described how her mind raced: "I need to just walk away from this. Wait, maybe I could find a way to get my boss to change. No, he would never do that. He's locked into who he is and who he's going to be. If I leave, someone will just take my place and earn this money, and I'll lose all the incidental benefits that I'm deriving from the situation."

Abby ultimately made the decision to stay, unwilling to give up the financial security and praise that came with her job.

She did come close to quitting once. She witnessed an incident with a client where the company owner's flagrant corruption and refusal to be held accountable caused real-world damage. She confronted him finally:

> I went into a meeting and I said, "This is wrong; this is absolutely wrong. I don't understand how you're not admitting fault on the part of the company. We have done damage, physical damage; someone could've been terribly hurt. We're so fortunate that no one was hurt or killed, and you are not facing up to our culpability. What is going on here?" And when I was told to shut up, I went back to my desk and I thought, "If I'm worth anything, if my morality, my idealism is real, I need to get up from this desk right now and quit." And I didn't. I swallowed hard and stayed.

From that point on, Abby was complicit in her boss's misdeeds and became privy to ever more opportunities for discomfort. "I would have to stand next to the owner as he stood in front of the company and announced there were just no profits this year, we'd all have to tighten our belts, and he'd have to cut salaries and benefits and let people go. Then he'd take me into his office and show me a picture of the new Porsche he'd just bought."

Abby concluded, "I stayed for twenty years, and I'd still be there if the owner hadn't died."

When Abby made her choice, she was forced to grapple with unpleasant realizations about herself. "I believed in always taking care of the little guy. Always being 100 percent honest, making the hard decisions to live a truthful life that would make my mom proud." Without skipping a beat, she admitted: "When it came down to survival and making money, I gave up that part of me. I thought I was this big noble, outstanding individual with a character made of steel and, well, guess what? No, I wasn't."

Looking back at her choices two years after leaving the company, Abby has no regrets. "It was totally worth it and I'd do it again," she said.

> Having no children, no spouse, I'm completely reliant on myself for income, for security. I'm not going to win the lottery. There's not going to be some huge windfall inheritance. I'm going to have to do what I have to do, and if that means letting go of my idealism in the workplace, so be it. The money is safety to me. I will compromise myself to make it. I see no difference between myself and a prostitute. I sold myself for money.

Although Abby felt justified in having put financial security first, she left her job with a sense of unease, as though the wealth she'd amassed was also a debt to others. She resolved to live strictly by her values moving forward. First, she was determined not to sugarcoat her choices. "My quest for truthfulness in my life includes talking about things that are unpalatable," she said. "I'd rather use a term like 'prag-matist.' But no, I was a sellout." She also has found a way to give back: using the money she made at her previous job to support herself, she works for a friend's small company whose ethics she finds far more palatable—for free.

Jeanette

Jeanette, who uses she/her pronouns, has always been moti-vated by security. In her ideal world, her job, finances, loved ones, and even life path would line up with predictability and plenty of safety nets. Raised in a religious, conserva-tive family in the Midwest, she believed in patriotism, ser-vice, trusting the system, and not making waves. She was a star athlete growing up. She went to law school and aspired to become an FBI agent. When told that she needed some career experience first, she joined the Air Force as an attor-ney in the Judge Advocate General (JAG) Corps, where she excelled.

The only problem was, Jeanette was gay. In the days of Don't Ask, Don't Tell, military personnel could be dis-charged if sufficient evidence could be found indicating an LGBTQ+ identity.[2] Although she'd been aware of her orien-tation since a young age and had had girlfriends since col-lege, Jeanette decided she would live a double life of sorts and make sure no one at work found out about her identity. In fact, she didn't even tell family or close friends she was gay until well into her military career.

Jeanette was eventually assigned the role of military prosecutor. Her job, in part, was to investigate claims of service members being LGBTQ+ and to prosecute and dis-charge them when evidence indicated this was in fact the case. The irony wasn't lost on Jeannette: she was helping fire members of her own community for holding an iden-tity that she shared but kept secret. "It was soul crushing at the end of the day because that could have been me. It still could be me," she reflected. Her work made her more aware than ever that she hated being closeted and not being able to bring her girlfriend to work events.

As she struggled to justify her actions, she prosecuted a gay man who came out in a fit of rage at his commander—he knew the rules and flaunted them in front of his commander. Jeanette mentally reframed her work as simply enforcing rules:

> I could rationalize that I'm just following the rules. I follow the rules, I know the rules, they're Don't Ask, Don't Tell. Once you tell, the rule is you gotta go. It's very a equals b, b equals c, a equals c, boom. So that's how I got there. I don't know how well it consoled me, but in the moment it was able to get me through.

Jeanette stayed at her job. She loved the camaraderie of the military and the way it felt like a large family. She felt comfortable and safe—the security factor—working for such a large and powerful organization. She liked her steady paycheck and the opportunities for travel. And she enjoyed the feeling of competence she felt there: she knew she was good at her job. After a few years, she was briefly switched to a defender role, arguing that the accused should not be discharged because the person was not gay or the evidence was insufficient. In this role, she'd protect LGBTQ+ people, not hurt them. But it lasted only a short while, and then she was switched back to prosecutor.

Jeanette eventually left the military after ten years working in her role and grappling with her feelings of complicity. The reason she left wasn't guilt but security: her job required that she move and she wanted to remain living with her girlfriend.

From the time Don't Ask, Don't Tell was introduced in 1993 to its repeal in 2011, over thirteen thousand service members were discharged for being LGBTQ+.[3]

After she left, Jeanette did have some regrets:

I wish I'd had more of a spine where I could have spoken up about a rule change. I don't know that I would have made it very far. There are people in the military who aren't just robots, as I was, and they are people who agitate, and they push people, and I'm impressed by that. I think I had an admiration for those people because they were stronger than I was. I wasn't willing to speak up because I was afraid I'd lose my job, and security was the end-all, be-all. If security is what drives you, then you're not going to agitate because if that security is lost, then you're lost. You're done.

Jeanette's new job was working for the federal prosecutor's office. (She initially applied to be a federal public defender but wasn't offered the job.) The vast majority of her colleagues were white men who had attended elite schools, and Jeanette felt like an imposter with something to prove. The problem was, proving herself meant being an effective prosecutor, and being an effective prosecutor, in Jeanette's eyes, resulted in destroying people's lives due to a criminal justice system she saw as deeply broken. Once again, Jeanette found herself complicit in a system she despised.

"I didn't want to be in the courtroom when the guilty verdict would come back, and invariably it would be guilty. And it just crushed me, it made me sad. These lives are crushed, they're broken. And I can't fix them, I just can't," she told us tearfully. "Being a piece of that is actually pretty challenging because you are a part of that infliction of harm. And I didn't want to inflict harm—I want to help people, and I didn't feel like the criminal justice system was a place where you could help people. I still don't think that it is." Hearing guilty verdicts hurt Jeanette's heart, but what hurt even more was seeing the devastating impact these verdicts had on the spouses and children of those she condemned. To do her job well, she had to ruin lives.

Jeanette believed that the people she prosecuted were worthy of redemption. These were people who had been hurt by others, who had been disadvantaged and abandoned by society, and who lacked the support they needed before they made the mistake that landed them in her courtrooms. Jeanette tried to affirm her belief through her work. When she could, she advocated for more time off for defendants and other small changes that would lessen the brunt of a guilty verdict, if only a little. Sometimes defendants would come up to her after a case and thank her—more than their own lawyers.

Eventually, Jeanette left that job: her wife started at a job far from the federal prosecutor's office, and Jeanette wanted to stay with her. With any luck, Jeanette's new job overseeing gender discrimination investigations will be a better fit for her values.

Reflection

Abby's and Jeanette's stories are about *honesty*. Both women found themselves in situations that not only compromised their values but caused real harm to others. By deciding to stay, each had to grapple with the implications of her choice on her personal value systems. Abby had to confront her belief that she would stick up for people being mistreated, and realized that, at least in the moment, her sense of justice was weaker than her desire for security. While Jeanette knew already how much she valued security, her experience illustrated just how far she would go for it.

We also noted how Abby embraced *accountability* after her experience. Rather than simply write off her selling-out experience as if it hadn't happened, Abby made the conscious decision to recognize how she had unbalanced her moral scales for money. Once she had what she wanted, she was responsible for making things right and rebalancing the scales—a commitment she put into action through her pro bono work.

See No Evil, Hear No Evil

The guilt of complicity is an uncomfortable feeling, and both Abby and Jeanette took substantial steps to avoid feeling it.

Abby had many opportunities to leave her job once she learned about the illegal activities at play, but as the days went by her moral smoke detector was left beeping. She had a responsibility to others at the company, especially the employees who had broken the news to her. She owed it to her company's clients, who were being harmed by the company's shady business practices. And she had her own belief in speaking out about injustice to uphold. When she made her choice to not only stay at the company but actively work to maintain the lie, she had to reckon every day with her moral failure.

In the short run, Abby managed her smoke detector by turning up the volume on the more appealing sounds around her. To drown out the noise from her compromise, she focused on the gains she achieved by staying at her job—praise, promotions, raises—and then she justified these gains by noting how difficult it was to support her boss and all he demanded of her.

Jeanette's discomfort from prosecuting people like her was also ever-present. However, rather than drown out the noise from her moral smoke detector with other sounds, Jeanette rationalized a reason to turn it off. If she was only enforcing the rules, then she faced no moral problem if the people she prosecuted had broken them.

In hindsight, Abby's and Jeanette's attempts to escape their problems seem especially apparent. Yet in the moment, such decisions can be far less clear. Abby probably never sat down at work and said to herself, "My morals don't matter as much as this paycheck." Jeanette didn't ask out loud, "How can I become more okay with helping discharge people like me from the military?" In fact, the strategies each used to mask her conflict seemed to explicitly make asking the real moral questions harder. Whether we like it or not, our brains are especially talented at smoothing over the difficulties we face. At times, this process gets in the way of the honesty we owe ourselves.

Making Things Right

When Abby left her company, she had to deal with twenty years' worth of unaddressed guilt. Her gains had come at the expense of her colleagues, her company's customers, and her own moral idealism. While she had left the situation, she could not take back what she had done. So she resolved to embody even more strictly her values and morals heading forward, compensating with more kindness, generosity, and earnestness. The one compromise she made would be balanced out by committing to living without compromise elsewhere.

When our actions cause harm, wanting to do one good deed to balance out the bad one is normal. Yet making a situation right isn't just about the external impact we have in the world but the internal impact we have on ourselves. Being complicit in harm can fundamentally shake our faith in our values. Healing this internal harm isn't as easy as engaging in one good deed. Like Abby, we may benefit best from a long-term commitment to working on ourselves.

Weathering Discomfort

Jeanette never spoke about leaving her jobs for moral or ethical reasons. In fact, the only reason she left any of her jobs was to stay with her partners: if her girlfriends had been fine with moving or staying put for Jeanette's sake, she probably never would have left any of the compromising positions she found herself in. To an extent, Jeanette tried to rationalize her situation so that she could feel less conflicted: she was just following the rules; she was helping defendants receive lighter sentences. Yet she knew that her justifications were flimsy. Jeanette bore nearly the full brunt of the discomfort from her choices.

Feeling the discomfort of an impossible choice, especially one where complicity is involved, is important. Discomfort helps you understand more about yourself and your values and can sometimes lead you toward making a necessary change.

Abby and Jeanette both told stories that on their face seem remarkable but in reality are commonplace. We all at some point or another find ourselves in situations that threaten not only our personal values but also our responsibilities to our communities and loved ones. We all have a price of staying; some amount of money, security, validation, or other benefits we crave is enough to buy our participation in genuinely harmful systems. Quantifying how much harm to yourself you're willing to bear to get what you want is difficult. Doing the same calculus for harm done to others is far harder.

Chapter 8

Seeking Balance

In the previous chapter, we told the stories of people who were torn between all that they loved about their jobs and a growing awareness that they were complicit in organizations that violated their ethics. These stories, as well as those that came before, are a reminder of the unrelenting ways our lives and circumstances invite us to compromise and sell out.

As we heard more of these stories, we wondered if any people out there have sought to strike a balance. Have they found a way to meet their personal needs and also live in line with their values? What would that even look like, and how do people's journeys change throughout their life span? In this chapter, we explore the stories of three people in different stages of their careers and how they worked to establish—and re-establish—balance in their lives.

Theo

Theo needed a job. The recent college graduate, who uses they/them pronouns, was several months into their search and was struggling to find a position that would affirm their values and beliefs. As a former student activist with programming experience, Theo initially thought that their talents could be put to good use in socially minded nonprofits and activist organizations. Yet Theo's brief experiences working in those settings had been unexpectedly traumatic.

"It felt like everyone was dependent on me," they described. "If I fail, I fail my communities and now people might die." Theo realized that they wouldn't be able to work sustainably in a high-pressure environment with real people's lives at stake and was looking for a different job that would let them live out their commitment to supporting disadvantaged communities.

They hated to admit it, but their top choice was at a large tech corporation. The job would more than pay the bills and offered low-stress work that they could mess up on: a missed deadline for a technical project with no social impact would never affect the marginalized communities Theo cared about. And the company was one of the few that invested in workers' mental health. It gave workers ample sick days, disability leave, and generous health coverage. Workers weren't expected to sacrifice their health for the sake of their work. This company sounded like an oasis in an industry where overwork, stress, and burnout are common. The problem was that it was tech. And activists don't have high-paying tech jobs—do they?

"I don't want to be a sellout," Theo explained. "I don't want to take all this wealth, which I only have access to because of my other privileges." Theo worried that other activists wouldn't see Theo's circumstances and would only see a white person who had attended an elite university earning buckets of money tinkering on an app that had nothing to do with social justice. Theo found it problematic to experience the privileges of a high income—earned from a job having nothing to do with social justice—while their identity and values were built around fighting for marginalized and disadvantaged communities. How could Theo justify such a decision to themselves and to their activist community?

Theo made an ambitious commitment to solve both problems at once. If they got the job, they would give away a large percentage of the money they earned:

> I created a very strict system for myself. I thought very hard about how much money it was ethical for me to keep. It was important to have an externally provided number for that instead of whatever I feel like, because I could probably justify anything to myself. What I settled on is that I keep the minimum amount to not qualify for housing assistance, and all the rest I redistribute with a focus on reparations, especially to Black, indigenous, and formally colonized communities. The story that I tell myself so I can sleep at night is that I'm not really selling out because I'm using my talent to access this wealth and then move it to places that need it.

Theo got the job. As they expected, working at a tech company that invested in its workers' mental health was

Reparations, defined as "the obligation of a wrongdoing party to redress the damage caused to the injured party," is perhaps best known in the context of slavery, in which case compensation would be offered to former slaves and their descendants. Reparations can also be understood as a form of giving back to one's community or to marginalized communities when one is in a position of wealth or privilege. In this latter context, the reparations are offered not in response to a concrete act against a specific other but rather in recognition that capital and privilege are often gained at the expense of marginalized groups.[1]

incredibly rewarding. "My workplace is an environment where I can take sick days when I'm sick; if I miss a deadline, nobody cares," Theo said. "People just say, 'Oh, I guess it was too aggressive a deadline; we'll move it back.'" That wasn't to say the job was easy. Theo was simply less concerned with stressing out over work-imposed deadlines that couldn't impact real people.

The job paid well. Staying true to their word, Theo began setting aside most of their income for donation. They opened another bank account and transferred a predetermined portion of each paycheck into it.

"I don't own that money," they explained. In their head, Theo was simply a temporary custodian of money that belonged to the people.

While maintaining the balance of all of Theo's personal, professional, and ethical needs has been tricky, they have been able to do so successfully with this job. "I always have a voice in my head saying, 'Theo, you're selling out. Theo you're selling out.' My actions are structured around having concrete evidence to say, 'Here are the specific ways in which I'm not selling out and the specific ways in which the life that I lead is in line with my ethics and morals.'"

Michelle

The 2008–2009 economic downturn was the largest to impact the United States since the Great Depression of the 1930s, and the company Michelle worked for was hit hard. Before the recession, the company, which ran a nationwide direct mail magazine that sold website design, business cards, and other products, was a strong partner to small businesses and their communities. This local focus is what drew Michelle, who uses she/her pronouns, to the work to begin with:

I worked for that company initially because I saw the opportunity to immerse myself in community. I really loved the opportunity to partner with small businesses: restaurants, hair salons, any business you might see in a strip mall in a community. I really liked talking with them about how to reach their target market and build their business. I had to walk into restaurants and know about restaurants, and I had to walk into a meeting with a construction guy and know a little bit about his business too, and I had to walk into a hair salon and understand a bit about that business and how it runs. I got to become a sort of jack-of-all-trades, and that's still useful to me now.

The 2008 recession, which began in the United States and ultimately devastated the global economy, was the worst financial crisis since the Great Depression of the 1930s. Banks, concerned that they would not be paid back, stopped offering the loans that most businesses depend on to survive. The United States lost two million jobs over the course of just four months in 2008, and consumer spending plummeted.[2]

At first, the recession didn't seem to have a huge impact on Michelle's daily work. But when it came to crunch time before one of the dozen mailing deadlines each year, Michelle realized two things: one, her company wasn't backing down on sales quotas, and two, small businesses weren't biting.

"It started being really important to meet last year's numbers," she recalled. "This was always the case, but last year's numbers were before the crash. This year, people are struggling to keep their doors open."

As the local businesses the company worked with did their best to stay afloat, Michelle tried to do her job even better. But at some point, it became impossible.

She realized she would be unable to meet last year's numbers without manipulating people out of their money—people who were struggling financially themselves. She went to her mentors in the company to tell them that the numbers weren't reasonable and that she'd have to coerce her customers to meet them.

"Sorry," one said. "This is the game. This is how it is."

Michelle quit, citing her values. "I had to walk away; I won't use my talent for that. It broke my heart that this company that I dedicated my life to for over six years sold its soul, became all about the numbers, and was no longer about partnerships with the local businesses at the forefront."

She went back to school, got a degree in political science, and sought work as a political science instructor. But as the months passed and she didn't get any job offers, she suspected that more than the recession was at play. On social media, Michelle talked openly about her political beliefs and work advocating for racial justice issues and movements. "I had two, three, four excellent interviews and I heard nothing, and then they went with someone else," she described. "I noticed the little things in interviews, like the moment where I say, 'Black Lives Matter' and they sit up a little straighter and blink a little harder."

Money was getting tight. To save costs, Michelle and her activist partner used their last few dollars to purchase an RV to live in, but even that didn't save enough money to allow her partner to support them both on his modest income. Michelle had to earn money, but she wasn't willing to work for another company that treated people like numbers. She decided to return to her marketing roots, this time providing the services herself—and eliminating the problematic middleman her company had been:

I've been trying hard to bring the skills that I gained in that corporate marketing world to the community. You can be a fitness instructor or librarian or teacher, but you still have to market yourself. You still have to sell yourself. You might be excellent at what you do or the most valuable person on the team, but if you can't sell yourself to that decision-maker, no one will ever know. I see my job as helping people with that aspect. You do what you do very well, you make an excellent pizza; let me help you tell the community you make an excellent pizza.

This work doesn't pay much, but it feels honest. For Michelle, who has stuck to her beliefs despite the consequences, it's a start.

Daniel

Born to progressive social activist parents, Daniel, who uses he/him pronouns, was raised from an early age believing in the need to make the world a better place. When he graduated college, his parents guided him toward a career of service work. But Daniel had his mind set on the burgeoning software business, a decision that his parents viewed as morally suspicious. "All businesses are evil because they're all just about themselves," they told him and tried to dissuade their son from going into the industry. Daniel, however, had already prepared a story for why this choice fit within their ethical framework:

At that time, microcomputers were going to be bringing power down to the people instead of being in big mainframes where they just belong to the CEOs. That was going to be a great equalizing event in and of itself. And because I was going to be involved in that whole part of the computer revolution, that was something that I could be proud of. I could stay true to how I grew up.

His parents grudgingly accepted his rationale. Daniel went into the software industry, started his own company creating digital trainings to bring power to the people as he had intended, and for several years was happy pursuing his dreams. But after five years of this, Daniel reached a crossroads. He was now married with young children, and the lifestyle he had pursued as an entrepreneur could not support his family. "I was living hand to mouth through angel investing," he explained. He needed to make a better living, but he still cherished the beliefs his parents had taught him. How would he square his values with his new family's financial needs? While speaking to a recruiter, Daniel shared his ideas about a career path that would fulfill all his needs. "I can find a company that has a socially responsible culture. I can have meaning and purpose, live my values, and have a good wage." The recruiter wasn't impressed:

> Why would you even think of working for socially responsible companies or nonprofits that have a good culture if you could work for the big tech companies? It's a more toxic environment, but you can make a bundle of money. You can really create value in the world afterward when you're rich, when you're in your forties or fifties, because then you did what you needed to do to put your kids through college. Why not just consider it two lifetimes: your first lifetime, three decades of your mercenary period, and then your second, when you can leave and do what you want with your charity? It might take you until your fifties, but then you can do it all.

Daniel wasn't sure if he could do what this recruiter was suggesting. He still believed in the power of technology to do good and wasn't willing to earn money if it meant he would be doing harm to the world. Then came his big break: a large company in the software business wanted to hire him to do what he was already doing but for much more money. Daniel took the job.

Unfortunately, working for this company turned out to be excruciating. The hours were brutal: oftentimes Daniel would return home at eleven o'clock or midnight, too late to say good night to his kids. The commute was long. And hardest of all, the culture was toxic. "It was a survival-of-the-fittest culture," Daniel explained. "You were rewarded for walking over the backs of others to get ahead, and that dynamic was set from the top." Caring about others, working for the good of the team, and being a compassionate employee not only put you behind but made you a target for others hoping to climb up. Daniel got the message loud and clear: "If you stick to your morals, it's hard to stay in the company. Sooner or later it's going to test you."

Daniel got his test. He was asked by his boss to lay off several of his direct reports, even though there were no performance-based reasons to do so. These were employees whom he had developed strong bonds with over their time working together, and as the layoff date loomed, they would approach Daniel before he left the office. "Am I on the list?" they asked. And Daniel couldn't answer them. HR had told him, "If you even tell them that they're on the list, we're going to fire you." Daniel had to stay quiet.

He stayed in that company for four years, motivated almost solely by the goal of sending his kids to college. "I chose to act as a mercenary and do this even though it meant that I didn't feel like I was being my best self at work," he shared. "If I had tried to do it for much longer, then it would have really affected my physical, mental, and spiritual well-being. So I was glad when I finally got out of there."

A century ago, college costs in the United States were kept low and often supplemented with endowments and gifts from the wealthy. This made sense at the time, since most college graduates went into the ministry or other low-paying, society-benefiting careers. That began to change in the early twentieth century when graduates began to seek high-earning careers. Student loans became an option for managing increasing tuition costs, which were raised even higher as the economy tanked due to the Great Depression. Tuition costs have steadily risen ever since,[3] rendering a college education unaffordable for many families. Currently, over one hundred colleges charge $50,000 or more for annual tuition.[4]

Daniel's next workplace, a smaller company, offered him a good deal: stock options. Daniel knew that when the company went public, the value of the stock would skyrocket. This payout would more than cover his children's college tuitions; it would allow him and his wife to live comfortably for the rest of their lives and even give back in the form of philanthropy. There was just one problem: Daniel learned that the leaders of this company cared about nothing but earning money and were willing to take advantage of consumers' trust to do so. Daniel's gut feeling was that he should leave. How could he be a part of this unethical behavior or condone it with his silence? But if he followed his gut and left after only three months, he wouldn't be able to take full advantage of the stock options he had received. It felt like an impossible choice between his values and his family.

Daniel consulted his wife and together they decided: Daniel would stick it out for the rest of that year and cash out with whatever he had then. It seemed like the best compromise between money and morals, but even so, remaining for an additional nine months was difficult. "It was an excruciating year," Daniel admitted. "I was basically serving myself over what was right, and what was right was to not be part of it. I thought, 'If I can wait twelve months, this will serve my family.'"

Daniel retired from the software business at age fifty, having successfully put his two children through college and secured financial stability for his family. One day, a friend forwarded him a job listing for a digital community builder at a mission-driven company working to make the world a better place. He took the job and almost immediately realized that this was what he had been missing:

> This company has now provided for me the most meaning and purpose in my life career-wise, after fourteen companies. It did actually come full circle from what I was doing in the first twenty years of my life to what I'm doing in my last twenty years of active employment. I do feel like there were definite work-related sellouts along the way, but I was conscious during the time of the trade-offs I was making on behalf of my family. I was at least thinking to myself, "These are not pure sellouts—I'm deciding to take a path that's nonoptimal to get to some higher path in the long range of my life."

When we met him, Daniel had been working at this new company for ten years. In his eyes, ending his career at the perfect company he had dreamed of joining many decades ago is nothing short of poetic.

Reflection

Theo's and Michelle's stories powerfully demonstrate *accountability*. More than anyone else we spoke with, these two individuals contextualized their actions in terms of their values and commitments and course-corrected when able. Theo's commitment to empowering marginalized communities led them to donate a sizeable chunk of their income. Michelle's commitments to supporting the local grassroots community led her to leave a stable career and stake everything on her community organizing work.

Daniel's story is the longest in this book. While many other stories focus on one selling-out decision, Daniel's discusses several over the course of his decades-long career. We were interested most in how he not only described his selling-out decisions in the moment but also spoke in great detail about how his values weathered his career trajectory. As his situation continued changing, Daniel's experiences embodied a willingness to experience *growth*. And even after his retirement at fifty, his surprising re-entry into the workforce to join the company of his dreams showed his ability to welcome *exploration*.

What Matters Most

In many ways, Michelle's and Daniel's stories are polar opposites. Michelle sacrificed much of what mainstream society values—money, comfort, and stability—to live the life she wanted to live. Daniel sacrificed things mainstream society encourages us to give up—time with his kids, his values, and parts of his ideology—to fulfill his financial responsibilities to his family. Yet their stories have surprising similarities as well. Michelle knew that sticking to her values would result in meaningful changes to her standard of living and consulted her partner before they made the choice together. Daniel knew that staying in an ethically dubious company would mean compromising his values and consulted with his wife before they made the choice together. Both made decisions almost solely on the basis of their moral compass: Michelle's read "grassroots organizing"; Daniel's read "family."

True to these compasses, Michelle would let almost nothing compromise her commitment to grassroots organizing, and Daniel would let almost nothing compromise his commitment to his family. The key word here is "almost." Michelle needed to make enough money to support herself. "How do I continue to do this work that is so important if I can't meet my own basic needs?" she wondered. Daniel needed to honor a promise that he had made to his father that he wouldn't pursue money out of greed. When we asked about this, he was adamant: "I made my commitment to my father that I wouldn't do that." Both found creative third options that allowed them, however imperfectly, to find balance between their morals and needs. Michelle's new business repurposes her skills to help her grassroots community, though her income is still low. Daniel was able to continue fulfilling his dream of bringing knowledge to the people through digitization, though his company didn't offer the best work environment. Despite the challenges that both experienced throughout their compromises, they don't regret the decisions they made.

A Balanced Life

Theo was able to make a creative decision that allowed them to live their values in a job many activists would view with disdain. The young professional effectively found balance at their first job out of college. Their story contrasts against

Michelle's, whose career trajectory spans a decade longer, and Daniel's, whose career has gone on for two of Theo's lifetimes. Daniel's experience was an insightful narrative involving many opportunities to sell out.

Like Theo, Daniel worked hard to make decisions in his life that served his values. Yet putting one's values first doesn't mean ignoring the challenges of living in a world that pushes people into compromise all the time. In the very beginning, he defended his compromise to go into the private sector by invoking the social good he could do through software. He defended his compromise to go mercenary by committing to improve his family's financial health. And he defended his compromise to stay silent in an ethically questionable organization with the hope of sending his daughters to college with the money. Each of these compromises made sense in the moment. But at the end of a long career, Daniel was aware that he had gone in a different direction than he had envisioned at the start. How far does it make sense to go to live according to one's morals?

What surprised us most was what Daniel chose to do after he retired. The company he joined in his midfifties—on a whim, no less—was the company he had idealistically described to the recruiter so many years earlier. It had a social justice mission. The company culture was amazing. And within his role he was able to exert a positive influence on the company and the world. As we heard Daniel describe his transformative experience there and the sense of contentment, meaning, and purpose he gained, we were moved by the idea of living a balanced life. We noted that Daniel did everything the recruiter recommended, but what truly gave him meaning wasn't philanthropy or charity but a job like the ones his parents had hoped decades ago that he would go into.

Chapter 9

What Makes a Sellout?

I mpossible choices. Smoke detectors. Painful compromises. We've explored more than a dozen selling-out stories and gotten a taste of the ways people handle some of the toughest choices they make in life. Some people lose their identities, others hide them, and still others make money off of theirs. Some try to get ahead, some try to stay afloat, and others take the hit. With so many stories and so many themes, we hope that you saw yourself in some of the people we spoke with.

In this chapter, we take a step back to reflect: What happened here? What were the experiences of selling out like, and why? And what can we glean from the stories we read so that we can all navigate the messy waters of selling out without sacrificing our integrity in the process?

Choices, Choices

What surprised us most was how many different kinds of choices people made to navigate sellout situations. Nearly everyone compromised in some way, but we saw tremendous variation and even creativity in how people went about doing it. Not only did their ultimate choices differ but also their motivations and whether they understood themselves as sellouts or not. Every impossible choice that people navigated was an interaction between an individual's *identities*, their *values and beliefs*, and the specific *situation*.

People's choices varied so much because they had different relationships to these three factors. A sellout decision made in a high-stakes situation but without much conflict between values and beliefs and identity will turn out very differently from a sellout decision made in a low-stakes situation but with a strong conflict between two identities.

Identities

The people we spoke with had a range of identities, but not every identity was important to every person, and not every person centered those identities within an impossible choice. Those who centered their identities in their sellout decisions typically had strong associations with them: their Blackness, their disability, and their queerness, as well as their identities as a fat person or activist.[1]

When we started writing this book, we expected to find much talk of selling out among the rich and privileged, since those are the stories often portrayed in the media. But interestingly enough, we found very few, if any, selling-out stories involving being able-bodied, high-income, or white. This isn't to say that people with socially advantaged identities don't go through these choices as well, because they certainly do. But for these people, the locus of conflict is more often about competing *values* rather than *identities*.

The reason for this is almost certainly because socially advantaged identities have the privilege of also being invisible when it's desirable. Most times people don't need to think about being rich, Christian, men, heterosexual, or able-bodied because they rarely encounter conflict due to these identities. On the other hand, minorities and marginalized groups are constantly thinking about identity because for many, identity is an extremely important part of their life.[2] This importance is what makes challenges to identity feel so impossible in the first place: you're less likely to see people stressed over less-important identities like "wine glass aficionado" or "Tetris player." For identities such as race, gender, class, religion, sexuality, and others, the real difficulties people may face in life—and the strong communities that often form in response to these difficulties—can add a gravitas to impossible choices that's no laughing matter.

Lose or even hide an identity and you risk losing the many things associated with it, such as personal meaning and a sense of community. When people make decisions based on identity, the choice can often feel far bigger because of how much there is to lose.

Beliefs and Values

Beliefs encompass your take on how the world works and your role within it, while values are about what you hold most dear in life. Beliefs and values are interesting because while they most certainly influence our behavior, our behavior influences them as well. Think about it: how did you come by the beliefs and values you have today? Most likely, you learned them from somewhere or someone. Over time, our individual beliefs and values solidify through many experiences but always remain susceptible to change.

All the people we talked with considered their beliefs and values in their sellout decisions. Some prioritized advocating for marginalized groups and believed strongly that they had a responsibility to do the right thing, while others valued security and believed that they had to look out for themselves first before anything else. And almost all of them valued authenticity—the feeling that they were being themselves, doing what made them feel comfortable, and living life in a way that felt true to them.

Many of these beliefs and values shaped how people perceived and handled impossible decisions. For example, people who felt the greatest responsibility to others seemed to struggle the most when they felt pushed to compromise, as they worried that by compromising they would be harming their community.

Circumstances/Situations

When we think about sellouts, we imagine people who look for opportunities and situations where they can sell out. But in reality, the situations usually find the people. A prediabetic health scare, a broken heater, a corrupt boss: none of these situations were predictable, yet they had tremendous influence on the decisions that followed. Practically every individual we spoke with except Jovan—who was trained to sell out from the very start—couldn't have anticipated the situations that would happen to them.

These situations had a considerable amount of influence over the decisions that people made. The higher the risk and the more immediate the choice, the more likely people were to compromise their values. Sellout crises, in particular, pulled for impulsive responses that may not have occurred in different contexts with less pressure and more time to think.

People were less likely to sell out in problematic ways when they could anticipate the decision in front of them and consider the best way to move forward. Consider the individuals in the stories on seeking balance. All of them considered their values carefully in the face of situational variables and constraints, and each came to a career decision that honored both.

We found it striking that in many cases, people said they didn't know how they would respond to sellout crises until they were actually in them. It's no coincidence that while we tend to think people sell out for personal gain, the majority of the people said they sold out to avoid loss.

The Internal Struggle

No one had an easy time making a decision to sell out. The conflict of grappling with impossible choices is perhaps one of the defining features of people's stories, but what moved us was how much people struggled to find the right path forward. Many described a grueling process involving lost sleep, fight-or-flight moments, anxiety, and indecision. Why is selling out so hard, even if deep inside we know what we need to do?

Self-Judgment

We're our own worst critic sometimes, especially when we think the situations we find ourselves in are somehow our fault. Oftentimes we make impossible choices harder by angrily judging ourselves for factors out of our control. Even if we made the best possible decision considering the circumstances, our moral smoke detector will go off time and time again. Many of the people we talked with struggled with feeling like a bad person as a result of not knowing the right decision or failing to adhere to their strict moral code. Some reacted with shame, as if they had failed irreparably by setting their moral smoke detector off in the first place. In fact, sometimes our indecision and self-criticism can be so extreme that they get in the way of our ability to move forward.

Rationalization

How do you know when your moral smoke detector has actually detected something versus when it's just given a false alarm? How do you know when to turn it off? We can be so good at telling ourselves the right things to quiet the beeping in our heads that sometimes we're not even aware that it happened. Is our rationale for doing or not doing something genuine or something we made up to deal with our discomfort? It's hard to know, so keeping ourselves honest leading up to and after impossible choices is extremely hard.

Fear of Change

Are you scared of change, loss, or failure? We suspect that many people, not just those we spoke with, worry at least somewhat about these things. To some extent, the more strongly individuals felt about their identities, their beliefs, and the communities they belonged to, the more frightened they were to contemplate potentially losing them or experiencing failure. Dreading change, especially if the impetus comes from the outside, was one of the most common experiences shared by the people we talked with. Change means that we could lose our sense of meaning or community. Change means we could even become different people with different values.

The Outside Storm

Circumstances and situations play a powerful role in people's impossible choices, even for people who on the surface may be thinking only about themselves when they make their decision. While the many people we spoke with all faced unique situations, a striking number of commonalities among them consistently pushed people in similar directions. Why did so many people face similar external pressures? Why did so many people share similar beliefs about the world and their obligations to it? And why, if people eventually arrived at a place of comfort with their choices, were other people sometimes so unhappy with those choices?

Culture Matters

While many of us may encounter similar difficulties in life, we most certainly don't all come from the same cultural backgrounds. Culture can have a significant impact on our values, roles, and obligations, as well as what situations we find ourselves in. An impossible choice for one person could be a no-brainer for another.

As we gathered interviews for this book, we spoke with many people whose full stories we didn't end up including. One of these individuals was Chris, a first-generation Chinese American whose parents immigrated with him to the United States when he was young. As we spoke with Chris, we learned that he was reluctant to give his own definition of selling out:

> Chinese culture is so focused on material excess and reputation. I'm first-generation and low-income, but my parents are always saying things like "You should become a doctor." In some communities, being a doctor for the pursuit of money is selling out, but that's not how they saw it. When I tell my parents that I want to try out banking after I graduate, they don't consider that selling out either. I think good fortune and prosperity are linked to wealth in so many instances of Chinese culture. I remember that when I got into Stanford, my parents said, "Your ancestors are looking after you." I can imagine this kind of genealogical heritage that starts at this baseline. My great-grandparents and grandparents were farmers in China. My parents owned a restaurant, so this line goes up slightly. Then I become a banker and the line goes up more. So much of the Chinese family's reputation is dependent on occupation and wealth.

Lily's experience as a Chinese American person reso-nates with Chris's. Her own understanding of selling out is complicated by the fact that she feels like she sold out to American individualism by pursuing a career she loved, rather than a career that would earn her wealth—the oppo-site of what one would expect based on how the culture at large discusses selling out.

We heard a related sentiment from our friend Vineet, who was born and raised in India and immigrated to the United States as an adult. In his case, the problem is that he didn't get married and have kids. Many in his local Bay Area community would not raise an eyebrow at such a life choice. However, from an Indian perspective, he says, this is a deeply selfish decision, ignoring what is often seen as an obligation and duty to his family and community.

Culture matters, especially when we look deeper into how different cultures and subcultures understand values such as integrity, authenticity, independence, and modesty. It shapes how we and our communities think of concepts such as wealth accumulation, social justice, and our individ-ual responsibility for the whole. It's one of the reasons why some people we spoke with made no mention of community judgment and others couldn't talk about anything else.

Whether a person was raised in a primarily individu-alist (valuing independence, self-reliance, and freedom of action) or a collectivist (prioritizing the needs of the group over those of the individual) culture can significantly impact where one's sense of obligation lies.[3] People from more col-lectivist cultures may weigh duty to their community more heavily than those from individualist cultures. In the United States, various racial/ethnic, religious, and socioeconomic subcultures display a wide range in terms of individualist versus collectivist values.[4] In this sense, our cultural values can strongly influence how, when, and why we choose to sell out, as well as how we view others who have made such compromises.

Getting Ahead

In the indie hit *Sorry to Bother You*, the Black, financially strapped main character, Cassius Green, takes a telemarketing job to save his home. He then learns that if he "talks white" on his calls, he's able to get ahead. He is so successful that he is promoted to "Power Caller," leaving behind his friends and breaking their strike to get to work himself. He finds out that the product he's become so successful at selling is deeply unethical but feels that it's too late to turn back. He's become so dependent on his wealth and comfort, as well as the praise that comes with being good at his job, that he's unwilling to let go.[5]

Many people feel suspicious of those who have compromised based on the assumption that compromise is a slippery slope. They feel that one compromise can lead to others until a person has completely given up one's identity or values and becomes someone unrecognizable, like Cassius Green. However, our experiences with our interviewees and folks in our own lives did not bear this out: people were most likely to sell out in a very specific circumstance while avoiding compromise in any other area or even compromising *less* in the rest of their lives to make up for the one area where they flexed their values. Likely this gap in perception versus reality is due to the common perception that selling out is a decision based on *character*, when at least as often, as we've established, it's based on *circumstance*.

In many societies around the world, success is viewed as a direct consequence of hard work within a meritocracy. If one subscribes to this belief, people who gain success without seeming to put in the right amount of hard work are seen as suspect. Paths to success that appear to skip or lessen the hard work can be perceived as cheating.[6]

While inequality has only grown over the last thirty years, Americans are still just as likely to believe that the United States is a meritocratic society where people are rewarded for their hard work.[7] Yet a sizable body of academic literature reveals that those with privileges—particularly wealth—have a fast-track to the American Dream.[8] Many of the most successful Americans today relied on means unavailable to others, such as parental loans, university legacies, and family connections. These shortcuts allowed them to gain entry into the privileged class through the opportunities generated by an elite education, prestigious job, and powerful connections.

People with one or more marginalized identities encounter obstacles of discrimination, prejudice, and exclusion that make competing on a level playing field an uphill battle. To compensate for these inequalities, they may seek to become more palatable to the privileged majority through straightening their hair, altering their name, or engaging in linguistic code-switching. It's striking that these marginalized shortcuts to success, taken in the face of discrimination and inequality, are often viewed as suspect by one's own community, while privileged shortcuts frequently go uncriticized.

In the chapters that follow, we'll return once again to the framework that opened this book. We've thoroughly explored the selling-out stories of seventeen people and unpacked how and why each one resolved a seemingly impossible choice. We've contextualized these many stories within the social, political, and economic contexts of each participant. And finally, we've shared our thoughts on which participants embodied which skills of our CHANGE framework.

In coming up with this framework, we also recognize that we didn't invent the wheel. None of these skills are new to you, and we don't intend them to be. Throughout the next few chapters, you'll learn how you can develop and use these familiar skills to tackle the challenges of selling out, with the help and expertise of the social scientists and experts who have come before us. The hard work of selling out more ethically isn't about trying to understand *what* it means to embrace honesty or growth, but rather *how*. Each chapter ahead will detail what it means to develop these skills and some of the challenges inherent in them.

We can't promise that these skills will definitely solve your problem or provide answers to the choice you've been agonizing over. But we do believe that the various parts of this CHANGE framework will give you plenty to think about and practice.

· Chapter 10 ·

Compassion

Our friend Donnovan is a grief counselor. Toward the end of a grief retreat weekend for bereaved fathers, the topic was self-care and self-compassion. One father described the conundrum he faced. This man had just lost his young child and he was reeling, unable to cope. He came to Donnovan with his own impossible choice: the grief retreat offered the healing and support he desperately needed, yet in choosing to go, he was leaving his devastated wife and surviving child at home, alone and drowning in their own grief and loss. He wanted to know which choice—going to the retreat or staying home with his family—was the compassionate one?

Donnovan's response was that compassion is not about what one chooses but rather how we treat ourselves when faced with a decision with equally hefty sacrifices on either side. Compassion comes in at the moment we realize we are faced with an impossible choice. Compassion is pausing to recognize the suffering that is caused by being pulled in different directions at once: "I'm suffering right now, this is so hard."

Compassion can also be used *after* making an impossible choice. If we make a decision and feel torn up about it afterward, Donnovan points out, we often interpret that to mean that we chose poorly. But so many choices involve pain and loss regardless of what decision is made, that continuing to suffer after a choice is not a sign you did the wrong thing. It simply means you made a hard choice and you're suffering and need compassion and tenderness.

The Pain of Selling Out

We've said it before, and we'll say it again: selling-out decisions are rarely easy to make, and we all struggle with them at some point. However, in many cases, to hold on to what is dear to us, something else must be sacrificed. Sometimes we must flex our identity or values to protect our health, our career, and so on. It's easy to stay focused on what was flexed, wondering who we really are after having made such a choice. Although this questioning process has its place, we must keep in mind what was at stake and why the decision was made to begin with. As we've seen, these decisions are commonly made under tough circumstances. We may be struggling with the marginalization associated with an important identity or find ourselves in an unfamiliar or unsafe situation. We may be forced to choose between the values that give us meaning and the goals that we've worked our whole lives toward. Compromising isn't failure. In fact, it's sometimes necessary for survival.

Given the context for many selling-out decisions, we can be unfairly hard on ourselves about the compromises we have made. We can feel pulled to rehash a situation over and over in our heads, imagining that if we think about it long enough, we'll see a better way out than the decision we made or are about to make. But often there is no better choice, and we then blame ourselves for compromising our integrity or authenticity. We tear ourselves down, filled with shame, guilt, or remorse. Or sometimes we blame others— or society as a whole—for the situation we found ourselves in, and maybe rightly so. But the unprocessed anger and resentment that can accompany such blaming have the power to tear us up as well.

For all these reasons, practicing compassion is an absolutely vital skill for selling out ethically. Without it, negative emotions can cloud the way we see ourselves and the decisions we've made. We can focus only on ourselves and miss the bigger picture and the external factors that pushed us into impossible choices in the first place. In this chapter, we'll explore what it means to practice compassion toward yourself and others and revisit some of the people whose stories you've read to see compassion in action. We'll also talk about fighting shame and imposter syndrome and the role of community.

Learning Self-Compassion

Dr. Kristen Neff is a world-renowned expert on self-compassion who has written multiple books on the topic and developed the self-compassion scale. She explains that self-compassion often starts with understanding compassion for others. To have compassion for others you must notice that they are suffering, be moved by that suffering to feel care and the desire to help them, offer understanding and kindness to them (rather than judging) when they fail or make mistakes, and recognize that suffering, failure, and imperfection are a part of the shared human experience. Self-compassion, Neff says, involves turning these kind and understanding feelings toward yourself:

> You may try to change in ways that allow you to be more healthy and happy, but this is done because you care about yourself, not because you are worthless and unacceptable as you are. Perhaps most importantly, having compassion for yourself means that you honor and accept your humanness. Things will not always go the way you want them to. You will encounter frustrations, losses will occur, you will make mistakes, bump up against your

limitations, fall short of your ideals. This is the human condition, a reality shared by all of us. The more you open your heart to this reality instead of constantly fighting against it, the more you will be able to feel compassion for yourself and all your fellow humans in the experience of life.[1]

Self-compassion has three primary elements, according to Neff. The first is *self-kindness versus self-judgment*, being warm and understanding with ourselves even when we make mistakes or things don't go according to plan. In the context of selling-out decisions, this means that even if you make a choice that has a negative impact on yourself or others, or that you realize doesn't fit with your values, you recognize that stumbling like this is a part of life, and you offer yourself sympathy and kindness rather than judgment.

The second element of self-compassion is *common humanity versus isolation*. Often, frustration in life comes with a strong sense of isolation, as though you are the only one struggling and suffering. Here, you see that suffering and mistakes are part of the shared human experience. You recognize that you are not alone; you are one of many who wrestle with your identities and values versus other things you want and need in life.

The third and last element is *mindfulness versus over-identification*. This means finding the balance between suppressing and exaggerating negative feelings when they come up. Recognizing the suffering of others can help with this, as well as observing negative thoughts and emotions with openness and clarity, neither denying them nor getting swept away by them. As you wade through difficult decisions around selling out and their aftermath, you acknowledge the pain, the sense of competing values and priorities, and new (not always flattering) information about yourself that may come as part of the process but without getting sucked down the rabbit hole about how hard it all is.

Self-compassion is not self-pity or self-indulgence, nor is it even self-esteem (although self-compassion can help build self-esteem). Self-compassion is simply a way of recognizing your humanness and being kind to yourself in the face of it.

Fighting Shame

Self-compassion is an effective antidote to the suffering created by many negative emotional states, including shame. Shame itself is an incredibly powerful and potentially damaging emotion. Whereas guilt is the feeling that you've *done* something wrong, shame is the feeling that you *are* something wrong, that something about you is flawed or inadequate. Feeling shame in response to a decision to sell out means that on some level, you worry that this decision reflects negatively on who you are as a person. Shame isn't always bad, of course. Feeling shame can be a response from your moral smoke detector that lets you know you did something that violates your moral and ethical system. However, many of us have a hair trigger for shame and we become convinced that we are deeply flawed despite a lack of any substantial evidence to that effect. In those cases, shame becomes a toxic emotion. To effectively fight shame, we need to understand why it happens.

In some ways, shame can be seen as an absence of self-compassion. It's the voice in our head speaking to our greatest and most secret fears and vulnerabilities. It's the words we've internalized from others in our life on how something about us is just not good enough. Dr. Brené Brown, in her book *Daring Greatly*, suggests that simply naming and speaking the ideas we're ashamed of takes power away from them. She writes, "If we own the story we get to narrate the ending."[2]

While perhaps a strange idea, shifting our thinking from shame to guilt can also be powerful. While guilt isn't a comfortable emotion by any means, it's a far more actionable one. "I failed" is a far more constructive thought than "I'm a failure."

The Role of Community

Isolation is powerful and toxic because it can serve to reinforce the negative individual and societal reactions to selling out. With no one to provide a reality check, small and even unconscious ideas that link selling out to being a bad person can spiral out of control. Finding community, especially communities of individuals who have made choices similar to the one you've made or are considering, is one of the most effective ways to fight shame.

Psychologically safe communities, or communities that you trust enough to be vulnerable in front of, are also able to provide critical feedback. Feedback can serve as a reality check. It can help you see that a decision was sound even though it left you full of doubt, and it can also help you to see the times you've ignored the consequences of a poor or potentially harmful decision.

Michelle, the grassroots organizer who wrestled with finding work that fit her values system, reflected on the power of a small, tight-knit community to give feedback:

> When we start to talk about how we want things to go and hold each other accountable to continuing whatever work is being done, we have way more of a chance of building institutions that won't ask us to compromise our

morals so much. It's very hard in the face of constantly being asked by the system to compromise your morals to remain steadfast, so having a core group of people who all have the same values and who all check each other with love is really crucial. It really comes down to love and trust and community.

Sometimes, however, we might not feel like we totally belong in our communities. One key culprit in this is imposter syndrome, the phenomenon of high achievers who internally feel like frauds. People of any identity and background can have imposter syndrome, though those who struggle with self-doubt are more vulnerable. Dr. Valerie Young, an expert on imposter syndrome and author of *The Secret Thoughts of Successful Women*, divides people into four "competence types," or sets of internal rules people hold that help create and maintain a lack of confidence: the Perfectionist, the Superwoman/man, the Natural Genius, and the Soloist.[3] Two of these, the Superwomen/man and the Soloist, seem especially germane to those struggling with selling-out decisions.

Superwomen/men (we'll just say *Superhumans*) are convinced they're phonies among classmates or colleagues who are the real thing. In response, they'll push to keep up and perform, often working harder and longer than those around them to prove their worth. Superhumans are relevant here because that feeling of needing to do twice as much to get half the credit is quite familiar to women, people of color, LGBTQ+ folks, and others who represent marginalized identities. This is important to point out, because the reason you feel like you're not enough may be because society has been telling you you're not enough. You don't have to swallow those messages without question. You *are* enough.

Soloists feel that they need to accomplish everything on their own and that asking for help is an indicator of being a failure or a phony. Soloists are relevant here for several reasons. First, again, if you represent a marginalized identity, you may feel more pressure to achieve without asking for help because you likely experience greater pressure to prove yourself and sometimes also represent your larger community. If you lean on a person with more privilege to get a project done, you may feel like you are reflecting a negative light on your identity. Second, operating in isolation can make values-based decisions, particularly selling-out decisions, more difficult and painful as well as increase a sense of shame. Finally, trying to achieve too much in isolation is unrealistic and, because of that, may make you feel more tempted or pressured to make decisions that don't fit with your values, leading to an even greater sense of being a phony and thus creating a vicious cycle.

Our colleague Dr. Meag-gan O'Reilly, a Stanford psychologist, offers a beautiful reframing of the imposter syndrome trap. She notes that people often feel most like imposters when they are doing something new. If you are the first in your family or community to go to college or have a competitive, high-paying job or branch out from traditional work into acting or the arts or entrepreneurship—or even if this path is just new to *you*—you are likely to feel less confident in your abilities and to wonder if you really belong. This is not because you're an imposter or a fraud, Dr. O'Reilly argues—it's because you're a *trailblazer*.[4] Trailblazing can bring with it plenty of self-doubt and shaken confidence, but it's also a courageous and important move that can bring many gifts to you and your family or community (even if they are shaking their heads at you right now).

So if you are plagued with self-doubt in your new school or job or with your other life choices, check to see if you may be trailblazing in some way. If so, you may not need to change yourself or your life path. Give yourself some credit for taking the risk of doing something new, and remember to practice self-compassion around the many mistakes you'll inevitably make along the way, as all of us make.

Compassion for Others

One of the great facets of self-compassion is that it leads to more compassion for others and vice versa. As we noted previously, everyone struggles and makes mistakes; it's part of our common humanity. Therefore, people around you struggle with sellout decisions and other impossible choices too and will occasionally make decisions in the service of self-preservation that you don't like. Be compassionate toward others as they wrestle with when and where to compromise (or not) and sometimes make terrible decisions along the way. As the famous couples therapist Dr. John Gottman likes to say, "We are all in the same soup."[5]

Compassion Enables CHANGE

We put compassion first in our framework because we believe that it is the fundamental prerequisite for everything else. To even begin the self-reflection required of honesty or the problem-solving required of accountability, you must first believe that as an individual you are worthy of love and care, that you aren't alone, and that your struggling is okay. Without compassion, the other skills of the CHANGE framework are nothing but coldhearted exercises.

Chapter 11

Honesty

One time, Inge was alone on a rather lengthy flight and she found herself sitting next to a rather chatty woman. Often Inge buries herself in a book during flights, but this time she was pleasantly drawn into a conversation about work, hobbies, and favorite foods. She was delighted at having found this new companion when the woman asked, "And what does your husband do?" Had we been in a movie, this would have been the moment when the music stops with an ugly screech.

Inge didn't have a husband. She had a girlfriend.

Inge gazed at the woman—who had a delicate gold cross hanging around her neck and a Chicken Soup for the Soul–type book clutched in her lap—and wondered if their lovely conversation would turn into hours of painful silence if she came out to her. Or was she judging her too quickly?

Inge made a split-second decision and offered a true but incomplete answer: "Oh, I'm not married," she replied, and left out the details.

Afterward, Inge felt uneasy about not saying more but reasoned that the situation was likely to have turned awkward if she had spoken up. Or maybe she was just taking the easy way out.

When we look at honesty as an attribute of an ethical sellout, it's not about the honesty of what Inge did or didn't tell the woman on the plane. Rather, it's the honesty of whether she's truthful with herself about what she did and why, as well as the impact of that choice. The lying to ourselves can keep us from living in line with our values and at peace with ourselves. In this chapter, we'll explore what's hard about being honest with ourselves, including some of the most common ways people rationalize their decisions to avoid seeing the full truth of them. When we peel away these rationalizations, we are able to better understand what we did, why we did it, and what the consequences were.

Brain Trouble

Our minds can be very creative in the ways they rationalize questionable decisions for us. Why are our brains so talented at pushing negative feelings like guilt, shame, and frustration under the surface when these very emotions can help us learn and grow as individuals?

Imagine that one day your moral smoke detector goes off, and you get information suggesting that one of your behaviors isn't matching up with your beliefs. For instance, perhaps you think of yourself as a generous person but you just crossed the street to avoid interacting with a homeless person. You might find that you feel awful: tense, distressed, guilty. Social psychologists call this cognitive dissonance, the negative state we feel when we hold two contradictory or clashing ideas, beliefs, or values.[1] Usually cognitive dissonance happens when we encounter something new that clashes with who we think we are. It's an uncomfortable feeling, and we're often motivated to reduce it by making sense of the new information. We can do this in five ways:

- We can use the new information and change our behavior to align with our beliefs or values: "I'm a generous person—I'll cross the street and give that homeless person a few dollars."

- We can use the new information and change our beliefs or values to align with our behavior: "I must not be a generous person."

- We can write off the new information by tweaking how we think about our beliefs or values: "I'm a generous person, but giving that person money is less effective than donating to a nonprofit organization."

- We can write off the new information by committing to other behaviors that support our beliefs or values: "I'll make sure to give more to the next homeless person I see."

- We can ignore or discount the new information: "I crossed the street because it was the fastest way to my destination, not because I wanted to avoid the homeless person."

All of these strategies reduce cognitive dissonance, but some are easier (and more tempting) than others. We tend to pick rationalization over other options because it doesn't require us to change anything but our interpretation. Changing behaviors takes work. Changing values and beliefs takes even more.

Reality-Testing Your Rationalizations

Rationalizations can help us ease feelings of guilt and shame over our choices, as well as help us see complicated problems as clearer and simpler. While these outcomes can be helpful, they complicate our efforts to be honest with ourselves. Below, we've listed some of the statements people make to themselves about selling out to feel better about their choice or mentally minimize its impact. Many of these statements reflect those Inge has heard from her clients and colleagues as they struggle to balance their needs and desires with their values. Each one is followed by specific examples and why a given rationale may mislead you.

- *The Long Game Rationale:* "I'm selling out in the short term so I can live my values in the long term" (i.e., It's okay that I'm compromising my values right now because it will set me up with the power, money, education, connections, etc. that I need to do the right thing later).

  Examples: "I'll work at this high-paying corporate job just until I make enough money to bail and work at a socially conscious nonprofit." "I won't say anything about the mistreatment of women in my company because it will interfere with my ability to move up; I'll wait until I'm in a power position myself and can make change from the inside."

  One problem is that people often get hooked on the money, power, and privilege once they have them, and then don't want to let them go. Temporary can become permanent. You may get invested in maintaining some aspects of the status quo because they benefit you too.

- *The Entitled Rationale:* "I've earned this after what I've been through" (i.e., Because I belong to a marginalized group or have suffered hardship, I get a free pass to be more self-serving).

  Examples: "I was raised poor, so I should get all the goods now, no matter what it takes or whose feet I step on." "As a woman in America, I've been through so much that I shouldn't have to answer to anyone."

  People who start out at a disadvantage often need to work twice as hard to get ahead. However, nothing in the past excuses you from taking responsibility for the present.

- *The Conformity Rationale:* "Everyone does it" or "If I didn't do it, someone else would" (i.e., My behavior is justified because it's so common, anyone in my place would make the same choice).

  Examples: "All the other Black folks at my company suck up to our racist boss and laugh at her offensive jokes, so I'm not going to be the one to stand up." "If I quit my job at the nuclear missile plant, they would just hire someone else."

  The problem here is that you might be circumventing responsibility based on what you see or imagine others doing. Other people's choices don't absolve you of responsibility for your own.

- *The Semantics Rationale:* "I'm not selling out; I'm just being pragmatic" (i.e., If I call it something else, it's no longer selling out).

  Examples: "Embellishing on my résumé isn't lying; it's just strategy." "Thinking about my own bottom line before I consider anything else is simply being realistic."

  Calling what you did something else doesn't change the impact of your actions. If you sold out, just acknowledge that you sold out.

- *The Trade-Offs Rationale:* "Does it matter how I got there as long as I got there?" (i.e., The ends justify the means).

  Examples: "So maybe I get tons of cosmetic surgery, which I don't even believe in, to keep this media job, but just think of all the girls out there who see me on screen and feel inspired." "I know I'm taking acting roles that promote horrible stereotypes of Asians, but at least there's an Asian on screen."

  The problem here is that success is not a zero-sum game: whatever you did to become successful is not automatically neutralized by your ability to get what you wanted. If you did something against your values, it's still against your values even if it got you where you wanted to go.

- *The Island Rationale:* "I just do my own thing and I don't worry what people think" (i.e., I'm not accountable to anyone).

  Examples: "So what if I got into college because my parents made a large donation to the school? It's no one's business how I got here."

  Like it or not, your choices and behaviors do impact others. Whether you owe a debt to your family or community may be up for debate, but even if you don't, you do owe others the consideration of taking into account how your decisions will affect them.

Honesty as a Path toward Accountability

When we make decisions, we may have a hard time acknowledging the true motivations behind them as well as their full impact. As we noted in the previous chapter, every choice has an associated cost. Sometimes that cost is to ourselves: a decision may show us that we are not who we thought or hoped we were. Other times, a decision may impact our friends, family, or community or people we don't even know. Selling-out decisions, in particular, have a cost. Although the payoff may be well worth it, the cost is still there, and we must first acknowledge it to be accountable for it. Accountability, addressed in the next chapter, is a big part of being an ethical sellout: it keeps us from being careless and irresponsible in our choices.

Before we can be accountable for our choices, we need to be honest with ourselves about them. Take a moment and think about the selling-out stories you've read. Were some people more honest with themselves than others about the motivations behind their decisions as well as their impact? Were some people too harsh with themselves for selling out?

Abby, who stayed in a job with an unethical owner, was tempted to tell herself that she was entitled to her ill-gotten raises and perks:

> The owner and I spent *so* much time together. I had singular access to his information. I was his babysitter and diaper changer. I spent so much of the day listening to him talk about his problems. He was a burden at every level, which added to my feeling that I earned this, which made me even more complicit. Letting him continue to exist in such a narcissistic, self-aggrandizing way made me more of a sellout. Instead of holding up a mirror, I just waited every Friday for my paycheck. I had plenty of choices. My white privilege gave me a thousand options. It's not like I needed this job to feed my children.

However, one of the commitments Abby has made to herself is not to sugarcoat her choices. "My quest for truthfulness in my life and my desire for it to be spread around the land includes talking about things that are unpalatable," she said. "I'd rather use a term like 'pragmatist.' But no, I was a sellout."

Being honest about the decisions we make means embracing to some extent the discomfort of cognitive dissonance. If you notice that you're rationalizing, congratulations—having the self-awareness to catch cognitive distortions is a crucial skill. If you can come to terms with the motivations behind your decisions as well as their potential impact, then you've done all the prerequisite work to be able to consider accountability.

Chapter 12

Accountability

Lily, while an undergraduate student, participated heavily in student activism. As part of a nonviolent protest against racism and police brutality, she joined dozens of students in blocking a major bridge. Everyone on the bridge that day was arrested, and Lily sat in the highway patrol office shaking: her legal documentation still read "male," and she didn't want to think about what would happen if she was placed in a men's prison. Lily was lucky to be among those released after her arrest; others went to jail that night. But the stress of her experience led her to turn her back on student activism.

For several months, Lily tried to justify her decision to leave as a reasonable response to the trauma she experienced. Yet she couldn't deny that some part of her was okay with avoiding accountability, repeating the same story about her protest and subsequent arrest as a "get out of jail free" card (irony intended) when talking about her lack of activism.

While Lily was wary of participating in grassroots protests that risked arrest, she was determined to find another way to remain accountable to the marginalized communities she had always fought for. Eventually she found a way to honor her commitment to social change in a way that made sense for her. By choosing a new direction for her academic studies, she was able to advocate for change in organizational settings and ultimately became a diversity, equity, and inclusion consultant.

A New Lens

What words and feelings come into your mind when you think about accountability? If you are like many of us, "anxiety," "pressure," "stress," "blame," or "punishment" may rise to the top. Accountability is frequently thought of as negative or punitive, a way of laying blame when something goes amiss. In truth, accountability can be a deeply vital and *positive* practice. It's about keeping commitments, being reliable, and taking responsibility for one's behavior. It's part and parcel of selling out ethically.[1]

In this chapter, we'll explore accountability through this positive lens. First, we'll take a look at how honesty sets up accountability and discuss how you can own the outcomes of your actions. Then we'll focus on ways you can proactively build accountability in your life through community support and personal commitments.

Owning Our Outcomes

In the previous chapter, we discussed the necessity of being honest about your motivations and reasons for selling out. Honesty plays an additional role in helping set up accountability. The first step of accountability involves recognizing the impacts of your choices on yourself and others. Doing so requires the honesty of self-awareness (asking yourself, "How do I feel after making this choice?") and the honesty of acknowledging impact (asking, "Does this choice harm others?").

More times than not, the answer to these questions is "I don't know." We may not always have clarity about our decision to sell out, especially after a sellout crisis or other decision made under pressure. We need to reflect on how we feel about our choice. This can look like sitting down and closing our eyes when we have a moment to think or writing in a journal about our thoughts. We also need to understand how others are impacted by our choice. This can look like having a conversation with trusted friends, asking for feedback from colleagues at work, or even doing research to better understand the larger context of a decision that had a community impact.

Accountability is about owning our outcomes, and more often than not it specifically refers to owning *bad* outcomes. We're often not concerned about accountability when we get what we want and everyone is happy. When things go wrong, however, accountability is about making them right again.

You will have a moment when you realize, with a sinking feeling, that your actions had an impact that you can't accept. There's almost always a way to make it better, whether directly or indirectly. Dr. Harriet Lerner, author of *Why Won't You Apologize?*, describes the importance of a sincere apology.[2] "More than anything, the hurt party wants us to listen carefully to their feelings, to validate their reality, to feel genuine regret and remorse, to carry some of the pain we've caused, and to make reparations as needed. They want us to really 'get it' and to make sure there will be no repeat performance," she explained in an interview with *Forbes*.[3]

As Lerner argues, the key point is to make it right. If emotions are frayed, this means reconnecting and repairing hurt relationships. If trust is lost, this means rebuilding trust through changed behavior. And if people have suffered as a result of your actions, this means fixing not only the emotional harm but also any physical and financial harm that may have occurred.

Following are several examples of taking responsibility.

Tanisha chose to go by a less obviously Black name for several years, until she realized she wasn't living an authentic life. This realization was an example of being honest with herself. The way that she took responsibility was by going back to using her real first name and then showing a willingness to share her journey—and what she learned—with others by writing a blog post about it.

Abby, who assisted a corrupt boss for her own gain, recognized the harm that her selfish actions had caused. Primarily to address her feelings of guilt, Abby resolved to take responsibility by working for free for as long as she was living off the money she had earned by selling out.

Inge's colleague Jana is a Black Caribbean woman who is proud of her racial heritage and her natural hair. She thought women who got weaves or straightened their hair were perhaps a bit less "woke" than her. However, when Jana got engaged, she suddenly wanted a long, flowing weave more than anything. After much internal debate, she got her weave. She loved it and had no regrets; the pictures looked fabulous. She realized, however, that she had been acting superior—woker than thou, if you will—toward people with weaves when she'd had her natural hair. Jana took responsibility: she acknowledged she'd been judgmental and vowed to respect all types of hair choices moving forward.

What we liked about Tanisha's, Abby's and Jana's stories of taking responsibility is that no shame was involved, no head-bowing or public apology or begging for forgiveness. These women simply observed that their behavior was not in line with their values, and they did something about it.

Front-Loading Accountability

One crucial part of accountability is making things right when you've messed up. Another key component is taking action to proactively build accountability into your life. While this can be done in many ways, we'll focus on two: finding community and living by a personal code.

Accountability and Community

Impossible choices and sellout decisions are personal decisions, not collective ones. No one can make your choice for you or force you to carry all the weight of your community—the decision is yours. That being said, accountability thrives best in a healthy community where members are able to hold each other accountable. The best communities provide support for the hardest of decisions in a few ways:

- *They support you unconditionally:* Unconditional support doesn't mean that people agree with everything you say or do but that they have your back no matter what. Supportive communities validate your humanity and recognize that your decision, regardless of its outcome, is an effort to find your way in the world.

- *They give honest feedback:* Communities can communicate feedback from a place of care and concern. They're on your side, and that's why they tell you what you need to know—even if it's uncomfortable. Communities have the power to see the big picture where you've gotten tunnel visioned in and let you know what they see. You might not like what your community may have to say, but this feedback can be valuable.

- *They offer conspiratorial support:* Communities can be a source of ideas too. When you're paralyzed before an impossible choice, sometimes the voices of your community can break the impasse and push you in the direction you need to go.

Even if you don't have a large community to support you, you can benefit from enlisting your friends, family, coworkers, or community to be your *accountability partners.*

Let's say that someone named Winona made a potential selling-out decision. Although she had no training or experience in indigenous medicine practices and her tribal ancestry was somewhat distant, she set up a practice as an "Indian spiritual healer," knowing that people tend to think Native women are natural healers. Winona could easily convince herself that she's making good money while doing no harm—unless she seeks out community. In this case, community looks like her grandmother, an accountability partner who is more in touch with indigenous medicine. By asking her grandmother about the implications of labeling herself an Indian spiritual healer, Winona learns what it actually means to be a medicine person in their culture and how claiming a healer title without training could harm both her clients and the reputation of traditional healers. After some reflection, Winona decided she really was drawn to becoming a spiritual healer, even if she wasn't yet ready to claim the title, and with her grandmother's help she sought out proper training and guidance.

Take another case, this time of Marcus, the first in his family to earn an advanced degree and have a white-collar professional job. Marcus found himself besieged by imposter syndrome. He was convinced that he had been a "diversity hire" who lacked the skills of his coworkers, that his work wasn't up to par, and that he wasn't truly contributing to the organization. Marcus could have decided to skate by, feeling too ashamed to confront his concerns about his performance but figuring he wouldn't get fired. Instead, he approached his manager and asked for an early performance review to serve as a reality check. To Marcus's surprise, he received positive feedback overall and a reminder that it takes time to learn all the ins and outs of a new job.

Accountability also thrives when you are open to others' feedback even when you didn't seek it out. Imagine that you're about to accept a job with a great salary and benefits, but the company has a questionable history of human rights practices in its overseas branch in India. You're excited about having landed the position, but your Indian friend points out that he's disappointed you'd agree to work for such a company. How do you respond?

It's important to recognize that the feedback may be valid, even if what your friend said is difficult to hear. He trusted you enough to be honest with you and he deserves some respect for that. Now it's up to you to take another look at your value system and your decisions. You may still opt to work for this company, but if you ignore its overseas practices, you're not being fully accountable for your decision.

Creating a Personal Code

As individuals, we have our own part to play when trying to build accountability in our lives. Developing a personal code of conduct allows you to fall back on your core values when making hard choices. Jovan, the Black college student who feels little to no stress from repeated decisions to sell out, benefited greatly from his internal code: "When the resources are meant for people like me and more deserving people aren't in the room, it's okay to sell out." Jovan's code outlined who he was accountable to (outside of himself), under what conditions he could practice accountability to them, and how to act outside of these conditions.

Creating your own personal code of conduct or inscribing "north" on your moral compass can be a powerful way to hold yourself accountable. As long as you're compassionate with yourself and honest about where your choices have led you, you'll be able to know when you've strayed and make things right.

Accountability is not a one-time thing. Accountability is a skill and value that you develop and maintain throughout your life. The bad news is that you're never done; the good news is that you don't need to have this skill nailed just yet. The more experience you have with practicing accountability, the more you'll also realize that your personal answers start seeming less black and white. Our journeys to practice accountability naturally take us to the next skill in our book: nuance.

Chapter 13

Nuance

Inge once had a therapy client, Jim, who was raised in a very strict, fundamentalist Christian household. As an adult, Jim was having marital problems and wound up having an affair. At first, he blamed his wife. "If you had given me what I needed, I wouldn't have had to look elsewhere," he told her. Eventually, his excuses and rationalizations broke down and he realized the full extent of what he had done. Instead of seeing himself as a good person who had made a problematic choice, however, Jim became convinced that since he had *done* something bad, he *was* bad—evil, in fact. Since the moral system he had been taught had no room for gray, a person was either flawlessly good or evil. "If a glass of water has a few drops of poison, we don't say that at least 98 percent of the water is pure," he declared. "If any of it is poisoned, it's all poisoned!" Regarding himself as morally poisoned due to having the affair, he could see no way out, no redemption. Instead of working on healing his marriage, Jim went into a spiral in which he struggled to justify his existence, given his new self-assigned identity as an evil adulterer.

Painting the world in simple terms of black and white or good and bad is tempting, but doing so has a significant downside. The problem with seeing yourself (or people in general) as either all good or all bad is that it leaves no room for change or growth—just categorization. Nuance is the opposite of this. Nuance makes room for people being flawed but still good, for difficult decisions with no clear right answer, for growing from mistakes, and for many, many ways to live any identity in this world.

In this chapter, we consider how dropping rigidity, purity, and black-and-white answers in favor of nuance and flexibility is a building block for selling out ethically. We'll take you on a walk from purity politics to nuance, and along the way we'll weave in some stories of people who have grappled with the pressure to subscribe to restrictive sets of rules for living their lives and what they did. Finally, we'll offer some tools for adding nuance to your life.

Purity Politics versus Nuance

Batman versus the Joker. Luke Skywalker versus Darth Vader. Harry Potter versus Lord Voldemort. The appeal of stories about good and evil is universal, and such stories almost always comes with a moral: be like the hero, lest you become the villain. Applying this black-and-white framework in real life is easy because of how deceptively simple it is. You're either a good person or a bad one, either normal or deviant, either a morally upstanding person or a sellout. Less common are stories where the hero makes questionable decisions or the villain has legitimate reasons for doing bad things. Why?

"Purity politics" refers to the idea that one can be 100 percent morally correct, that there is no room for flexibility or compromise, that there is one correct way to live on this planet without causing harm. Purity politics are common in communities around the world, from progressive and activist circles, where the focus is on what it looks like to be a good person of color, queer person, feminist, or activist, to conservative faith communities, where flexibility in life choices can be seen as an indicator of overly pliable morals.

Tanisha, the entrepreneur who changed her name to sound less Black, describes how purity politics in Black communities can make people feel like they need to check racial checkboxes to be a "good Black person":

> Some Black people believe that in order for you to be a good Black person, you should be tweeting about injustices and reading Malcolm X and wearing your natural hair. You should be speaking out against the patriarchal white society, and you should be celebrating Kwanzaa, and if you don't do all these things then you're not a good Black person. That's problematic, because what if you're Muslim? If you don't meet those things, then you're not Black. If you don't watch these movies, watch these shows, support these initiatives, you're not Black. And I think that that's out of fear, because we feel like we don't have an ally if they don't subscribe to the same things or check all the checkboxes on the list.

Similarly, former first lady Michelle Obama wrote in her book *Becoming*, "Speaking a certain way—the 'white' way, as some would have it—was perceived as a betrayal, as being uppity, as somehow denying our culture."[1]

Tanisha believes that these purity politics (and identity policing) originate from historical situations where it was necessary to band together as a community to survive or overcome oppression. In those cases, making sure everyone was on the same side and of the same mind was necessary because being able to count on each other was life or death. Under purity politics, people who are not members of an identity group are suspect and should be held at arm's length (therefore, dating, collaborations, or other close relationships with people who hold different—generally more privileged—identities create a weakness for one's own group and imply questionable loyalties).

For instance, Chris, a college student, felt judged when he told his classmates, many of whom were first-generation college students, about his planned career choice:

> When I tell my friends that I want to be a banker, some of my first-gen friends give me this disgusted look, like "You're going to commit yourself to making money instead of fighting for justice, instead of fighting for discrimination or marginalized people?" I don't really see things in black and white, and that kind of argument that my friends make—it's either sell out or fight for your people—I think that's a hyperbolic statement and a big exaggeration. It's way more complicated than what they're making it to be.

There will always be reasons why we don't entirely fit into the expectations of ourselves and of our social groups. Knowing from the start that we can never be a model or perfect member of any group will allow us to more easily make the choices we need to.

In an interview with the *Atlantic*, Alexis Shotwell, author of *Against Purity*, makes the case that "personal purity is simultaneously inadequate, impossible, *and* politically dangerous for shared projects of living on earth."[2] She explains some of the problems with purity as a goal: "Every ethical system we have starts from the view that we're all in the world with other beings, we're embedded in the broader world. We're connected, we're implicated, and that's why we need to think about ethics."[3] As people wrestle with that reality, they often turn to what they can do individually, thinking, "I can at least work on my own responsibility or choices." The problem with this, Shotwell argues, is first that it's impossible: one cannot live a life completely pure, completely free of participation in racial injustice or global warming or whatever the issue of concern is. Second, focusing on individual purity isn't especially useful. "It doesn't do us any good to aim for individual purity," Shotwell states.

> When we start doing that, we become solipsistic, we become narcissistic, we become very focused on our own personal little thingy and that means that we don't aim to make systemic, bigger changes. Aiming for that kind of individual absolution—as soon as we mess up, and as soon as someone points out that we're actually still connected and implicated, we might be tempted to give up at that point.[4]

Shotwell continues:

> On the left, a lot of the time what happens is that people try to have only the right words, the right views, the right lines. They develop a kind of party line that they try to hold on to, and then spend quite a bit of time disciplining other people's behavior and speech. It's not that we want to say harmful things or have bad views. But this turns into purity politics when that self-monitoring or disciplining other people's speech or behavior is all we end up doing.
>
> So we need to figure out: What does a politics of imperfection look like? What happens if messing up is not the worst thing that could happen?[5]

Shotwell feels that moving away from personal purity means two things. One is having an attitude of self-forgiveness: we can mess up and still move on and be helpful. "Giving up personal purity allows us to confront the possibility of being shamed and not have that destroy us."

If you're doing antiracism work, especially if you're a white person, you're going to mess up and someone's going to say that you're racist. What happens if that doesn't mean you never do any antiracism work again? Instead you say, "I did a racist thing, I messed that up, let me figure out how I can repair." Which doesn't mean getting the kind and generous person of color, probably a person of color, who told you you did a racist thing, to work it through with you.[6]

(If this attitude of self-forgiveness feels familiar, that's with good reason. It's a lot like the self-compassion we discussed previously.)

Shotwell states that giving up personal purity also liberates us from feeling like we have to do everything ourselves. We are not going to be able to solve a whole lot of problems personally, but there are some we can personally work on. Shotwell refers to this as distributed ethics. "The ethical obligation becomes not 'How am I going to solve all these huge and enormous things,' but instead, 'What can I work on? What's within my reach? What am I connected to?'"[7]

Let us repeat: the perfect woman or Black person or queer or trans or disabled or fill-in-the-blank person does not exist. This is true for all of us but especially for people who hold marginalized identities, because tension will always exist between what those in our community value and what the larger society values, and both of these sets of values and expectations will inevitably be somewhat out of line with who we uniquely and authentically are.

Mahogany, the Black woman who kept quiet to pass her doctoral psychology class, found herself in the midst of these tensions when she sought out a church for her family: should she stay with her Black church despite its homophobia or move to a church that isn't predominantly Black but is more affirming of a variety of identities?

I stopped going to the church in South Central because of its homophobic stance. But then, when I went back to visit over the summer, there was pain in their eyes because I have the fluidity to go. And now I go to a wealthy church that reps people that are disabled and that are trans and that are different ethnicities. They're marching for people that are illegal immigrants. And they're marching for LGBT and everything. And I don't wanna raise my daughter hating people that are queer, 'cause her mom's queer. But now she's away from a mainly Black church.

Mahogany switched churches but not without a pang of loss knowing her daughter won't be raised in a Black church the way she herself was. As someone navigating multiple identities, she knew the dilemma was, literally, more than black and white.

However, she found herself making the opposite choice when it came to housing:

You always want to affirm your integrity. I live in a Black neighborhood with a white husband. I could've run off and lived in Venice if we were looking at a mainly white area or Santa Monica, or I could disappear in a Beverly Hills area. But I would have felt like I was selling out.

It's difficult to try to thread the needle though. I've had my house burglarized, twice, and I've had people come in my house four times. And two of the times they were successful at taking a lot out. And so my stance to live in a Black neighborhood and not behind a gate, I question it. But it's ironic, because now I put commercial-grade steel bars on my windows for me to feel safe to stay in my Black neighborhood. And so, I didn't wanna live behind a gate in a community that's gated, but my house now is like a fortress.

We won't leave with the advice to simply be one's authentic self because that's trite and simplistic. We already know that identity is fluid and that who we are in this moment may change next week or next month and also that how we present or carry out our identities may vary based on setting. Sometimes all those selves are equally real and authentic, and sometimes we need to turn the dial up or down on something for pragmatic reasons, and that's okay too.

Focusing on the Bigger Picture

Making a sellout decision almost inevitably involves a clash between values, desires, or goals that one holds dear. Once again, there is no choice without a loss. Therefore, rather than trying to find a solution or way out in which loss is avoided, it makes more sense to step back and look at the conundrum in the moment in the context of the bigger picture. First, pull in the skills you've already learned from previous chapters.

- Treat yourself with compassion as you wrestle with your decision.

- Pause to ensure you are being fully honest with yourself about your motivations and the potential impact of your decision.

- Consider how you might front-load accountability into the choice you make.

Now, ask yourself the following questions to build nuance into your skillset:

- *Whom does this choice impact most?*

- *What is lost and gained in making this choice?*

- *What values are involved in this choice? Which ones are being prioritized?*

- *Is this a choice that just looks bad (poor optics) or one that may cause actual harm?*

- *Who, if anyone, may be harmed if I make this choice?*

- *Will this choice result in a bigger gain that seems to outweigh any possible harm?*

- *Whom will this choice matter to in five years?*

Nuance helps promote honesty and accountability. We can feel tempted to avoid honesty with ourselves because we are afraid of encountering the full truth of our actions and motivations. However, nuance allows us to see the complexity of the decisions we make and move beyond believing that complicated dilemmas have simple answers. Doing so helps turn off a misfiring moral smoke detector. Nuance also allows us to move toward greater accountability through approaching our responsibilities and obligations more realistically. When what we're accountable for feels manageable, we are more inclined to welcome personal accountability.

Chapter 14

Growth

Rachel was at one of the lowest points of her life. Her workplace had been unresponsive to her requests for urgent accommodations for her disability, so she decided to take on the company legally. On behalf of herself and others who needed protection, she filed a claim of disability discrimination. The federal commission that heard her complaint believed it had merit and was pursuing it. This was an opportunity to create change at a national level that could create protections for her and also countless others with disabilities. But Rachel was ill, exhausted, and depleted. As much as she wanted to keep fighting, she realized that if she did, "there would be nothing left of me to fight for." So, facing what felt like an impossible choice, she dropped the claim and reluctantly went on an unpaid leave.

Rachel didn't expect what came next: "I have had the most glorious period of spiritual, emotional, psychological, and physical growth," she observed with wonder. She's aware of a new ability to live in the moment and an ability to see herself as having inherent value regardless of what she's doing. She's months away from her agreed-upon return-to-work date, and she has no idea whether her job will be able to accommodate her. "However," she said, "my growth has allowed me to not get too worried about that; I am confident the best solution will present itself."

The crisis moments in our lives when we are faced with seemingly impossible decisions often feel painful in the moment, but they are also opportunities to change and grow. In this chapter, we'll consider some ways to open up room for growth in your life, including how to embrace change, move toward a growth mindset, reconnect with your values, and sit with discomfort.

Embracing Your Changing Identities, Roles, and Expectations

Selling out can sound like a one-time deal, but in reality we are faced with such choices every day. Our identities, as well as the roles and expectations attached to them, are in flux all the time. Seeing change as continuous growth rather than betrayal, regression, or self-destruction helps us make the best of our choices and circumstances. Stay open-minded: where we end up after selling out is no more permanent than where we started. We can and will keep changing.

Growth versus Fixed Mindset

We can thank Dr. Carol Dweck, in her book *Mindset*, for contributing greatly to our current concepts of growth and fixed mindsets.[1] With a fixed mindset, we believe that we are either good at something or not. Everything is about inherent ability. With a growth mindset, we believe that we can develop skills through practice and effort. A fixed mindset says that if the outcome was poor for you, you failed; a growth mindset says that if the outcome was poor for you, you have an opportunity to learn.

As a society, we tend to believe in effortless accomplishment rather than achievement that comes through effort. We imagine our heroes as superhumans who naturally tended toward greatness. Think of your greatest hero, someone you truly admire. Do you assume that person got where they are with minimal effort, purely due to natural gifts? We may tend to remember Martin Luther King's "I Have a Dream" speech and forget about the beatings and jailings that he endured. A common misconception is that success is a smooth upward journey when in reality it entails many setbacks. Aspiring actors may find themselves playing the lead in a Broadway play one day and an elf in a suburban mall the next. We encourage you to research your hero's backstory. Chances are, you will find that tremendous effort went into their success—and now you can admire them all the more for it. To paraphrase Oscar Wilde, experience is simply the name we give to our mistakes.

A growth mindset is crucial because it builds resilience around our inevitable mistakes and failures, and it serves as a reminder that we are continually growing and developing as people.

Staying Connected to Community, Culture, and Ritual

So much can change in the process of making what seems like an impossible choice. Crises and loss can lead to growth, but rapid periods of growth can also be disorienting and stressful. In such times, holding on to some constants and routines can be helpful. If you're fortunate enough to remain connected to a strong and supportive community, maintain contact with it as much as possible. Even if you've made choices that you're less than proud of, give others the opportunity to offer you a more supportive and noncritical voice. If you don't belong in your old community anymore, that's okay too. You can find and create new community, which we'll talk about in the next chapter. Also, the loss of one community is not necessarily the loss of all communities. Most of us have community in our family, our work, or our academic world or perhaps in faith, athletics, or other activities. When we lose one community, we might focus on the others in our life.

In addition to community, the constancy and enduring nature of culture and ritual can be reassuring. Perhaps certain foods, customs, or music evoke a comforting sense of home or connection to your roots. Eating macaroni and cheese or dancing the samba may provide you with a feeling of connection. Maybe now is the time to find the soul food restaurant, pride parade, or dance group that will bring you a sense of self-awareness and belonging.

Perhaps you find a particular ritual soothing: having a nightly cup of tea or a yearly gathering of friends to watch the Super Bowl. Making your special sweet potato casserole for Thanksgiving or taking a weekly walk with a friend. Be sure to make time for it. Routines and rituals can serve as positive anchors when everything else is in flux.

Reconnecting with Your Values

Try to understand your motivations for selling out in the first place. Before you judge yourself for your choices, think about all the factors that may pull you in one direction or another. This can provide helpful information about your values and priorities—not what you think they should be but what they actually *are*. The following list includes the values that were articulated as motivators by people who shared their stories with us. Which of these areas has been a primary pull for you in the past? How about right now?

- Authenticity
- Material gain or prosperity
- Community acceptance
- Loss avoidance

- Social justice
- Social recognition
- Career success
- Personal health and well-being
- Health and well-being of your family and loved ones
- Security

What's tough about values is that we rarely are motivated by just one. Not only that, but the ones that rank highest for us on a good day may not be the ones that rise to the top when we're in crisis. Our values can be just as fluid and flexible as the rest of our identities, and with good reason: as we've seen, they are often pitted against one another in impossible choice situations. Like it or not, we are often forced to flex values that are near and dear to our hearts.

Sitting with Discomfort

Life offers plenty of opportunities to learn to deal with distress, and that is especially true in the context of sellout situations. Distress in your life may arise from your moral smoke detector going off, life changes due to your responses to impossible choices, or other factors both in and outside of your control. Learning to sit with distress and discomfort is an important life skill. Often in our society, distress is seen as a problem to be fixed, a sign of something wrong. We rush to move out of our distress. Sometimes nothing is wrong: times of transition often involve growing pains.

When you feel upset or distressed, take a moment to pause before acting. Soothing yourself can help you get clear on whether there is actually a problem to be fixed or whether the distress itself is the problem. A good place to start is by practicing self-compassion: notice that you are struggling and that you need kindness. See if you can discern what you need in this moment, which often differs from what you think you *should* need. If your thoughts are murky or going in circles, then writing or talking with someone you trust may have a clarifying effect. Breathe. Get some sleep.

Inge's mother, Marcia Cebulska, discusses the value of writing in her upcoming book, *Skywriting*:

> On our worst days, our pasts can feel like a bewildering jungle of hurt and shame; our present like a fog of indecision; and our futures, a brick wall of impossibility. Writing can help tame our past, focus our present, and give us a hand in creating the path of our future. Writing can help us see the storylines of our lives.
>
> Working toward seeing the threads of our lives as a story can help us see patterns, recognize and affirm our individuality, and embrace our gifts.[2]

Marcia reflects:

> What I've learned is that writing helps me. Writing down the story of what happened or what might happen can lift me off the treadmill of anxiety. Writing can take a circular gerbil wheel of worry and give it at least the appearance of a beginning, middle, and ending. It can smash the circle of worry into a more manageable line. One can write down the story of what's happened so far, list alternatives, record the advice of one's inner sage.
>
> It may not solve the actual issue in this very moment but, at the least, it can help lift it off one's mind so one might just get the bit of rest needed to figure out a solution, approach, or attitude the next day.[3]

After you have a chance to soothe yourself, you may find that no action is necessary at all; you just needed to attend to your distress for a period of time. Or perhaps there is a problem that still needs fixing: with a calmer head, you'll be in a better place to determine next steps.

Thinking Small

Sometimes you know that it's time to make a change in your life, but you feel terrified to move outside the familiar. Or maybe you're in the middle of a significant life transition and the level of distress is overwhelming.

Baby steps, small actions that will get you closer to where you want to be, can help move you out of a stuck place. For instance, if you're considering a career change, you can research options, set up informational interviews, and talk with a career counselor—all without committing to a decision one way or the other.

Perhaps you're already in the midst of an intense growth or transition process and it has a momentum of its own. It's also helpful to think small in such a situation. The focus may be on what can at least bring you joy or decrease your suffering while life is in flux.

Chapter 15

Exploration

In a photo from one of the first times Inge's family visited California, she (about four years old) and her dad are on the beach, shoes off, pants rolled up. She's holding her father's hand as he pulls her toward the waves and she leans back toward shore.

That photo, Inge leaning away from the ocean but letting her dad lead her to it, captures the ambivalence she still has (and maybe we all have at times) around exploration. Looks exciting—but is it dangerous? Can I back out if I change my mind? Can I try it just a little bit?

We grow throughout our entire lives and especially after making significant life decisions. Growth brings with it the potential to change and explore, and we urge you to embrace it. In this chapter, we frame exploration as the final skill needed to sell out ethically. We will introduce the concept of the beginner's mind as a foundation for positive exploration. We will revisit the idea that your identities are fluid that you may need to find new community, culture, and ritual when they change.

Beginner's Mind

Exploration means opening ourselves up to new ideas, experiences, and ways of living. We are experimenting. Inevitably, some experiments will work better than others. If you try some things that don't work for you, no worries. Exploration is not about winning or always guessing right, but instead about openness.

A powerful way to create that openness is to bring yourself into what Zen Buddhists call the beginner's mind. In the words of the Zen monk Shunryu Suzuki, "In the beginner's mind there are many possibilities; in the expert's mind there are few."[1] This refers to having a sense of possibility, eagerness, and openness when engaging in an activity, even if it's something you've done countless times before. For instance, most of us learned to walk so long ago that we barely notice ourselves doing it. If you imagine yourself as a small child who is just learning to walk, however, each step holds meaning and wonder.

Sellout situations provide a great opportunity for you to be in a beginner's mind. You are already there, in unexplored terrain full of flux and change. You are no longer an expert in some areas of your life; you are a novice. We discussed in the previous chapter how taking accountability for our choices can stimulate personal growth. We can take this even further, especially with the choices that change our life trajectory. Imagine embracing this newness and your own lack of knowledge and preconceptions about where you've just landed. Imagine exploring this new direction of your life with wonder and a sense of possibility.

Flourishing in the Face of Change

One of the most powerful implications of selling out ethically over the course of a lifetime is the potential for our decisions to point us in new and unexpected directions. Over our personal journeys, we may find that things that we previously believed to be essential parts of ourselves no longer feel important, and things that used to feel unimportant now feel essential.

People previously thought of identities as static and unchanging. Social scientists now recognize that most identities contain an aspect of fluidity—even those with a biological component.[2] As your physical and emotional selves interact with the world, the world will change you just as you will change it. So it makes no sense to try to hold on to a previous version of yourself that no longer fits. Fat people become thin, atheists become religious, straight people become queer, men become women, disabilities can be reversed, and so on (and vice versa). The bad news is that this leaves very few things certain. The good news is that this leaves a great deal of your life open to exploration.

Identity fluidity can be a heady subject to embrace because we have no clear image of what it looks like in our minds. Should we be trying on new religions every day? Should we be trying to constantly change who we are? Fortunately, that's not what we're suggesting. Embracing identity fluidity is about recognizing that even fundamental aspects of ourselves can change and welcoming these changes as they happen.

Often one of the hardest challenges of a new identity or life direction is parting with what's been left behind, and selling-out decisions are no different. Maybe you can't claim a community as your own anymore, or you don't feel you have the right to. Maybe your new job or school or neighborhood means that you can't keep up with familiar habits, like watching your favorite show with your crew or Thursday night drinks or Saturday yoga, the things that help you to feel comfortable and connected. Maybe you could still take part in those activities if you wanted, but it turns out that you just don't want to anymore. These changes, although they're an inevitable by-product of growth, can leave you feeling unmoored.

Sometimes your community is no longer a positive force in your life. Maybe the people around you simply cannot understand your decisions or some part of your identity, despite your efforts to try to stay connected and help them understand your perspective. Or you've come to realize that your community is toxic in some way or doesn't share your values. Or perhaps one result of your choices is that you no longer belong to your old community because your identities or experiences have changed.

In situations like these, seeking out new community can be vital. Finding people who share your experiences and your newfound identities can be extremely validating and powerful.

We're not of the opinion that most empty spaces should be immediately filled. Rather, they offer a great opportunity to explore your options. Sometimes idealizing your previous life can be tempting—everything was so simple back then! But if you're making changes, you're likely doing it for a reason. Take some time to engage with different possibilities and try them on, rather than rushing to replace your previous life.

When seeking new community, think about what your goals are. Do you crave the connection of close confidants? Hangout buddies to join you in activities? People who share your values and priorities? People who have a certain identity or experience in common with you? Or perhaps all of the above? Whatever is on the top of your list can offer some guidance as to where to look.

In a moving essay (titled, tellingly, "The Only Metric of Success That Really Matters Is the One We Ignore"), Jenny Anderson writes about building community:

> What I would come to learn, slowly, is that community is about a series of small choices and everyday actions: how to spend a Saturday, what to do when a neighbor falls ill, how to make time when there is none. Knowing others and being known; investing in somewhere instead

of trying to be everywhere. Communities are built, like Legos, one brick at a time. There's no hack.[3]

If you feel lost about who your community is now, it may be time to create something new. Despite its downsides, social media can be a useful place to find (or create) a group of others who, for instance, also left working-class upbringings to pursue elite educations or who are also reeling after getting bariatric surgery or who also capitalized on some aspect of their identity and need to process it. You may feel completely alone, but these people may just get you. Seek out events that correspond to your passions and interests and you're likely to come across some kindred spirits.

Maybe you've got your people but your life is different now. Why not explore new ways of living it? Rituals can be anything from a weekly outing to practices that feel deeply personal and spiritual, but what they have in common is that they refuel you and help you feel more *you*. Why not move a bit outside your comfort zone and develop some new rituals to try out? Take some time before letting yourself settle into a new routine. Try different things, explore, and take note of how you feel. This could look like taking a class in an area of interest, joining a Meetup group, volunteering for a cause close to your heart, or simply introducing yourself to new people in circles you already inhabit, such as work or school or social events.

Conclusion

"I can sell out ethically." Try that sentence on for size, feel it on your tongue. What feelings come up as you say it? You might find it strangely refreshing. Or you might find that familiar discomfort rising up, a product of our society's ardent dislike of sellouts and sympathizers. You might still think of traitors, of hypocrites, of politicians gone rogue, of musicians who have lost their edge. But we hope that you also think of a graduate student gazing at a picture of her family wondering if she should retake a class, a young professional pondering how much money is enough to donate, and a closeted prosecutor agonizing over verdicts.

At the end of our journey through impossible choices of identity, beliefs, and values, through circumstances both unbelievable and utterly mundane, we've shared a glimpse of the many ways in which we all compromise and sell out in our lives. We've outlined a framework of skills—CHANGE—that you can use in your life to help navigate the before and after of impossible choices and manage the squawking of your moral smoke detector. Hopefully we've also expanded the idea in your mind of what it means to sell out, planted the idea there that perhaps you've sold out at some point too, and made the case that perhaps that's not such a bad thing.

At the start of this book, we described the context for selling-out decisions and what can make them so challenging:

1. An economic, social, and political system that makes selling-out dilemmas almost inevitable

2. A tendency to believe we are alone when we grapple with these dilemmas

3. Conflicts between our values, beliefs, duties, and obligations that can be so challenging we refer to them as "impossible choices"

4. A somewhat faulty, unreliable system for guiding us through these ethical dilemmas, which often lets us know we've made a mistake only after the fact

By now you've witnessed the process of over a dozen people as they wrestled with these decisions, and you likely have your own thoughts about their experiences. You've seen the systemic and contextual factors at play. You've noticed the times people were comforted by community and the times they felt alone or even judged by those they counted on to support them. You've observed their dilemmas as they realized the potential sacrifices required to get their wants and needs met. And finally, you've seen their responses when their choices don't fit with their own moral systems. We asserted at the beginning that while selling out is often viewed as a moral failure, it is in fact nuanced decision-making in the context of a seemingly impossible choice.

We hope we've been clear that although nearly everyone sells out, not all selling out is ethical. The six skills of our CHANGE framework—compassion, honesty, accountability, nuance, growth, and exploration—are tools that you can use to maintain your integrity in a world filled with opportunities to compromise. Yet these skills are far from a checklist; they collectively form a set of principles for living our best lives. Compassion lays the groundwork to respect ourselves and those around us. Honesty helps us gain self-awareness and realize how our actions shape the world around us. Accountability gives us space to act when—and not if—we stray from our values. Nuance helps us see beyond the black and white to make hard choices in hard circumstances. Growth allows us to learn from our mistakes to become better people. And exploration helps us continually evolve throughout our lifetimes to take on the challenges we'll face. Where these skills will take you is up to you. We close with a manifesto that sums up our thoughts on selling out ethically:

"Whatever my identities, beliefs, or values are, I get to determine for myself how to hold them and express myself to the world. I get to determine whether I want more safety, comfort, or well-being at any point and to own those desires. I commit to being kind to myself and my challenges, honest with myself about my motivations, and accountable for my behavior and making things right when I've done wrong. I commit to being open to flexibility, growth, and exploration, to take up space in the world, and to live my life with integrity."

The path forward is not certain and never will be. We hope that this book helps you find your way.

Notes

Chapter 1: Framing CHANGE

1. Jann S. Wenner, "Lennon Remembers, Part One," *Rolling Stone*, January 21, 1971, https://www.rollingstone.com/music/music-news/lennon-remembers-part-one-186693/.
2. Deborah A. Prentice and Dale T. Miller, "Pluralistic Ignorance and Alcohol Use on Campus: Some Consequences of Misperceiving the Social Norm," *Journal of Personality and Social Psychology* 64, no. 2 (1993): 243.

Chapter 2: The Stranger in the Mirror

1. Michael Hobbes, "Everything You Know about Obesity Is Wrong," HuffPost, September 19, 2018, https://highline.huffingtonpost.com/articles/en/everything-you-know-about-obesity-is-wrong/.
2. Joy Wilke, "Nearly Half in U.S. Remain Worried about Their Weight," Gallup.com, July 25, 2014, https://news.gallup.com/poll/174089/nearly-half-remain-worried-weight.aspx.
3. American Psychological Association, "Fat Shaming in the Doctor's Office Can Be Mentally and Physically Harmful: Health Care Providers May Offer Weight Loss Advice in Place of Medical Treatment, Researchers Say," ScienceDaily, August 3, 2017, www.sciencedaily.com/releases/2017/08/170803092015.htm.
4. Sara Goering, "Rethinking Disability: The Social Model of Disability and Chronic Disease," *Current Reviews in Musculoskeletal Medicine* 8, no. 2 (2015): 134–138.
5. J. D. Vance, *Hillbilly Elegy* (New York: HarperCollins, 2016), 30.
6. Evan Greer, "Powerful Gay Rights Groups Excluded Trans People for Decades—Leaving Them Vulnerable to Trump's Attack," *Washington Post*, October 29, 2018, https://www.washingtonpost.com/outlook/2018/10/29 trumps-attack-trans-people-should-be-wake-up-call-mainstream-gay-rights-movement/.
7. Michael Ervin, "The Last Hours of William O'Neal," *Chicago Reader*, January 25, 1990, https://www.chicagoreader.com/chicago/the-last-hours-of-william-oneal/Content?oid=875101.

Chapter 3: In and out of the Closet

1. Letitia Slabu et al., "Trait and State Authenticity across Cultures," *Journal of Cross-Cultural Psychology* 45, no. 9 (2014): 1347–1373.
2. Marianne Bertrand and Sendhil Mullainathan, "Are Emily and Greg More Employable Than Lakisha and Jamal? A Field Experiment on Labor Market Discrimination," *American Economic Review* 94, no. 4 (2004): 991–1013.
3. Catherine Hill et al., *Barriers and Bias: The Status of Women in Leadership* (Washington, DC: American Association of University Women, 2016).

4. Sharyn Graham Davies, "The Transcendent Bissu, Aeon, March 28, 2019, https://aeon.co/essays/the-west-can-learn-from-southeast-asias-transgender-heritage.

5. "Feminizing Hormone Therapy," Mayo Clinic, October 07, 2017, https://www.mayoclinic.org/tests-procedures/mtf-hormone-therapy/about/pac-20385096.

6. Allyson Hobbs, *A Chosen Exile: A History of Racial Passing in American Life* (Cambridge, MA: Harvard University Press, 2014).

7. De Elizabeth, "J. K. Rowling Explains the Reason behind Her Pen Name," *Teen Vogue*, July 10, 2017, https://www.teenvogue.com/story/jk-rowling-reason-pen-name.

8. Lesley Milroy and Pieter Muysken, eds., *One Speaker, Two Languages: Cross-Disciplinary Perspectives on Code-Switching* (Cambridge: Cambridge University Press, 1995).

9. Michelle Obama, *Becoming* (New York: Crown, 2018), 94.

Chapter 4: It's Mine to Sell

1. Holly Yan, "What We Know So Far in the College Admissions Cheating Scandal," CNN, March 19, 2019, https://www.cnn.com/2019/03/13/us/what-we-know-college-admissions-cheating-scandal/index.html.

2. Madison Park, "What the College Cheating Scandal Says about Race," CNN, March 14, 2019, https://www.cnn.com/2019/03/14/us/college-admission-affirmative-action-race/index.html.

3. Sandy E. James et al., *The Report of the 2015 U.S. Transgender Survey* (Washington, DC: National Center for Transgender Equality, 2016).

4. "The Empathy Gap between White Social Workers and Clients of Color," USC Suzanne Dworak-Peck School of Social Work, https://dworakpeck.usc.edu/news/the-empathy-gap-between-white-social-workers-and-clients-of-color.

5. Chloe Cheng, "Defining Diversity: LGBTQ Faculty Often Find Themselves outside the Bounds," *Daily Pennsylvanian*, April 26, 2016, https://www.thedp.com/article/2016/04/lgbtq-scholarship-versus-faculty.

6. Abigail J. Stewart and Virginia Valian, *An Inclusive Academy: Achieving Diversity and Excellence* (Cambridge, MA: MIT Press, 2018).

7. "Biography," Congressman Markwayne Mullin, accessed January 11, 2017, https://mullin.house.gov/biography/.

8. "Cherokee Nation Honors U.S. Rep. Mullin," *Times Record*, updated January 4, 2013, https://www.swtimes.com/sections/news/politics/cherokee-nation-honors-us-rep-mullin.html.

9. Chris Casteel, "Cherokee Nation Chief Calls President Obama Best President Ever for American Indians," NewsOK, updated September 4, 2012, https://newsok.com/article/3707011/cherokee-nation-chief-calls-president-obama-best-president-ever-for-american-indians?page=2.

10. Sean Murphy, "Okla. GOP Candidate Mullin Got $370K in Stimulus," KXII News 12, September 6, 2012, https://www.kxii.com/home/headlines/Okla-GOP-candidate-Mullin-got-370K-in-stimulus-168842676.html.

Notes

11. Aura Bogado, "Why Does Congress's Only Cherokee Member Keep Voting against VAWA?" *Nation*, March 1, 2013, https://www.thenation.com/article/why-does-congresss-only-cherokee-member-keep-voting-against-vawa/.

12. Valerie Volcovici, "Trump Advisors Aim to Privatize Oil-Rich Indian Reservations," Reuters, December 5, 2016, https://www.reuters.com/article/us-usa-trump-tribes-insight/trump-advisors-aim-to-privatize-oil-rich-indian-reservations-idUSKBN13U1B1.

13. Levi Rickert, "Cherokee Congressman Markwayne Mullin Calls Trail of Tears a 'Voluntary Walk,'" Native News Online, November 2, 2018, https://nativenewsonline.net/currents/cherokee-congressman-markwayne-mullin-calls-trail-of-tears-a-voluntary-walk/.

14. Twila Barnes, "Did Markwayne Mullin Forget Who He Is?" Indian Country Today, March 18, 2013, https://newsmaven.io/indiancountrytoday/archive/did-markwayne-mullin-forget-who-he-is-4yoLEVFIdkq-ahYGUdoZcw/.

15. Louis Fowler, "Trump Has His Scouts: Markwayne Mullin and the Native Sellout," The Lost Ogle, November 8, 2018, 2018, https://www.thelostogle.com/2018/11/08/trump-has-his-scouts-markwayne-mullin-and-the-native-sellout/.

16. Karen Biestman, Interview by authors, Palo Alto, CA, December 12, 2018.

17. Valerie Taliman, "Lakota Declaration of War," The People's Paths, accessed March 28, 2019, http://www.thepeoplespaths.net/articles/warlakot.htm.

18. Alice Emily Marwick, "Selling Your Self: Online Identity in the Age of a Commodified Internet" (PhD diss., University of Washington, 2005).

19. William M. Denevan, "The Pristine Myth: The Landscape of the Americas in 1492," *Annals of the Association of American Geographers* 82, no. 3 (1992): 369–385.

20. Valerie Wilson and Zane Mokhiber, "2016 ACS Shows Stubbornly High Native American Poverty and Different Degrees of Economic Well-Being for Asian Ethnic Groups," Economic Policy Institute, September 15, 2017, https://www.epi.org/blog/2016-acs-shows-stubbornly-high-native-american-poverty-and-different-degrees-of-economic-well-being-for-asian-ethnic-groups/.

21. Srividya Ramasubramanian and Mary Beth Oliver, "Activating and Suppressing Hostile and Benevolent Racism: Evidence for Comparative Media Stereotyping," *Media Psychology* 9, no. 3 (2007): 623–646.

22. Chuck Culpepper, "Florida State's Unusual Bond with Seminole Tribe Puts Mascot Debate in a Different Light," *Washington Post*, December 29, 2014, https://www.washingtonpost.com/sports/colleges/florida-states-unusual-bond-with-seminole-tribe-puts-mascot-debate-in-a-different-light/2014/12/29/5386841a-8eea-11e4-ba53-a477d66580ed_story.html.

Chapter 5: The Sellout Crisis

1. Leah Donnella, "'Racial Impostor Syndrome': Here Are Your Stories," NPR, January 17, 2018, https://www.npr.org/sections/codeswitch/2018/01/17/578386796/racial-impostor-syndrome-here-are-your-stories.
2. Rudolph P. Byrd, Johnnetta Betsch Cole, and Beverly Guy-Sheftall, *I Am Your Sister: Collected and Unpublished Writings of Audre Lorde* (New York: Oxford University Press, 2009), 226; and Stevenson Jacobs, "Rastafarians Struggle with Discrimination," WWRN, July 15, 2003, https://wwrn.org/articles/5335/.
3. Noel Gutierrez-Morfin, "U.S. Court Rules Dreadlock Ban during Hiring Process Is Legal," NBC News, September 21, 2016, https://www.nbcnews.com/news/nbcblk/u-s-court-rules-dreadlock-ban-during-hiring-process-legal-n652211.
4. Byrd, Cole, and Guy-Sheftall, *I Am Your Sister*, 226–227.
5. Byrd, Cole, and Guy-Sheftall, 227.
6. Michael Chui, Susan Lund, and Peter Gumbel, "How Will Automation Affect Jobs, Skills, and Wages?" McKinsey & Company, March 2018, https://www.mckinsey.com/featured-insights/future-of-work/how-will-automation-affect-jobs-skills-and-wages.
7. Ken Eisold, "Unreliable Memory," *Psychology Today*, March 12, 2012, https://www.psychologytoday.com/us/blog/hidden-motives/201203/unreliable-memory.

Chapter 6: The Greater Good

1. Erica, J. Hurley and Lawrence H. Gerstein, "The Multiculturally and Internationally Competent Mental Health Professional," in *Internationalizing Multiculturalism: Expanding Professional Competencies in a Globalized World*, ed. Rodney L. Lowman (Washington, DC: American Psychological Association, 2013), 227–254.
2. Carolyn I. Rodriguez et al., "The Role of Culture in Psychodynamic Psychotherapy: Parallel Process Resulting from Cultural Similarities between Patient and Therapist," *American Journal of Psychiatry* 165, no. 11 (2008): 1402–1406.
3. Gloria Wong et al., "The What, the Why, and the How: A Review of Racial Microaggressions Research in Psychology," *Race and Social Problems* 6, no. 2 (2014): 181–200.
4. Christa Marshall, "Will the Midwest Turn Its Back on Addressing Climate Change?" *New York Times*, June 4, 2010, https://archive.nytimes.com/www.nytimes.com/cwire/2010/06/04/04climatewire-will-the-midwest-turn-its-back-on-addressing-86784.html.

Chapter 7: Dancing with Complicity

1. "Corruption Perceptions Index 2018," Transparency International, January 29, 2019, https://www.transparency.org/cpi2018.
2. *Encyclopaedia Britannica*, s.v. "Don't Ask, Don't Tell," updated September 24, 2018, https://www.britannica.com/event/Dont-Ask-Dont-Tell.
3. Gary J. Gates, "Discharges under the Don't Ask, Don't Tell Policy: Women and Racial/Ethnic Minorities" (Los Angeles: Williams Institute, 2010).

Notes

Chapter 8: Seeking Balance

1. Nadra Kareem Nittle, "The Debate over Reparations for Slavery in the United States," ThoughtCo, updated January 26, 2018, https://www.thoughtco.com/reparations-debate-4144738.
2. *Encyclopaedia Britannica*, s.v. "The Financial Crisis of 2008," by Joel Havemann, February 2, 2009, https://www.britannica.com/topic/Financial-Crisis-of-2008-The-1484264.
3. Lily Rothman, "Putting the Rising Cost of College in Perspective," *Time*, August 31, 2016, http://time.com/4472261/college-cost-history/.
4. Farren Powell, "See the Average Cost of Attending College in 2018–2019," *U.S. News & World Report*, September 10, 2018, https://www.usnews.com/education/best-colleges/articles/paying-for-college-infographic.

Chapter 9: What Makes a Sellout

1. Richard Jenkins, *Social Identity*, 4th ed. (New York: Routledge, 2014).
2. Dominic Abrams, and Michael A. Hogg, "Comments on the Motivational Status of Self-Esteem in Social Identity and Intergroup Discrimination," *European Journal of Social Psychology* 18, no. 4 (1988): 317–334.
3. Hazel R. Markus and Shinobu Kitayama, "Culture and the Self: Implications for Cognition, Emotion, and Motivation," *Psychological Review* 98, no. 2 (1991): 224.
4. Daphna Oyserman, Heather M. Coon, and Markus Kemmelmeier, "Rethinking Individualism and Collectivism: Evaluation of Theoretical Assumptions and Meta-Analyses." *Psychological Bulletin* 128, no. 1 (2002): 3.
5. *Sorry to Bother You*, directed by Boots Riley (Los Angeles: Annapurna Pictures, 2018).
6. Matthew O. Hunt, "Religion, Race/Ethnicity, and Beliefs about Poverty," *Social Science Quarterly* 83, no. 3 (2002): 810–831.
7. Marianne Cooper, "The False Promise of Meritocracy," *Atlantic*, December 1, 2015, https://www.theatlantic.com/business/archive/2015/12/meritocracy/418074/.
8. Richard V. Reeves, *Dream Hoarders: How the American Upper Middle Class Is Leaving Everyone Else in the Dust, Why That Is a Problem, and What to Do about It* (Washington, DC: Brookings Institution Press, 2018).

Chapter 10: Compassion

1. Kristin Neff, "Definition of Self-Compassion," Self-Compassion, accessed May 11, 2019, https://self-compassion.org/the-three-elements-of-self-compassion-z/.
2. Brené Brown, *Daring Greatly: How the Courage to Be Vulnerable Transforms the Way We Live, Love, Parent, and Lead* (New York: Penguin, 2015), 80.
3. Valerie Young, *The Secret Thoughts of Successful Women: Why Capable People Suffer from the Impostor Syndrome and How to Thrive in Spite of It* (New York: Crown Business, 2011).
4. Meag-gan O'Reilly, interview by authors, Palo Alto, CA, September 30, 2018.

5. John Gottman and Julie Schwartz Gottman, *And Baby Makes Three: The Six-Step Plan for Preserving Marital Intimacy and Rekindling Romance after Baby Arrives* (New York: Harmony, 2008), 6.

Chapter 11: Honesty

1. Leon Festinger, *A Theory of Cognitive Dissonance* (Stanford, CA: Stanford University Press, 1957).

Chapter 12: Accountability

1. Henry J. Evans, *Winning with Accountability: The Secret Language of High-Performing Organizations* (Dallas: CornerStone Leadership Institute, 2008).
2. Harrier Lerner, *Why Won't You Apologize? Healing Big Betrayals and Everyday Hurts* (New York: Touchstone, 2017).
3. Kathy Caprino, "Why Won't You Apologize? Relationship Expert Harriet Lerner Teaches Us How," *Forbes*, January 12, 2017, https://www.forbes .com/sites/kathycaprino/2017/01/12/why-wont-you-apologize -relationship-expert-harriet-lerner-teaches-us-how/.

Chapter 13: Nuance

1. Michelle Obama, *Becoming* (New York: Crown, 2018), 40.
2. Alexis Shotwell, *Against Purity: Living Ethically in Compromised Times* (Minneapolis: University of Minnesota Press, 2016).
3. Julie Beck, "The Folly of 'Purity Politics,'" *Atlantic*, January 20, 2017, https://www.theatlantic.com/health/archive/2017/01/purity-politics /513704/.
4. Beck.
5. Beck.
6. Beck.
7. Beck.

Chapter 14: Growth

1. Carol S. Dweck, *Mindset: The New Psychology of Success* (New York: Random House Digital, 2008).
2. Marcia Cebulska, *Skywriting* (Topeka, KS: Flint Hills Publishing, forthcoming).
3. Cebulska.

Chapter 15: Exploration

1. Shunryu Suzuki, *Zen Mind, Beginner's Mind: Informal Talks on Zen Meditation and Practice* (Boston: Shambhala Publications, 2010), 2.
2. Daniel Wiese et al., "The Fluidity of Biosocial Identity and the Effects of Place, Space, and Time," *Social Science & Medicine* 198 (2018): 46–52.
3. Jenny Anderson, "The Only Metric of Success That Really Matters Is the One We Ignore," Quartz, March 12, 2019, https://qz.com/1570179 /how-to-make-friends-build-a-community-and-create-the-life-you-want/.

Acknowledgments

The authors would like to thank:

Our interviewees: Sophie, Julia, Tanisha, Shyen, Jovan, Lam, Beth, Ben, Mahogany, Diana, Abby, Jeanette, Theo, Michelle, Daniel; Jana, Chris, Vineet, and Alan; and finally those we interviewed whose stories ultimately didn't make it into the book. Thank you for sharing your time as well as some of the most difficult and messy moments of your lives with us. We hope we did your stories justice.

Jeevan Sivasubramaniam, editor, for getting us started, and Anna Leinberger, editor, for seeing us through to the end. We're also grateful to the entire BK Team for hosting us on Author Day, one of the most exhilarating, enlightening, and exhausting experiences of our lives.

Claire, Kasie, Donnovan, Rachel, Meag-gan, Alex, Tom, and all the others who reviewed, contributed to, and offered feedback on our book.

Lily would like to thank:

Rich, Sascha, Andrea, and Kristen for editing, advice, love, and support.

Danger, Crystal, and Melissa for a home outside of home when I needed a break.

Inge, my coauthor, for her vision and initiative that set this book in motion.

My parents, for supporting me even after I chose a career that wasn't computer science (sorry!).

Yrie and Ranna for being cats and walking all over my laptop when I wanted to write.

Red Rock Coffee, for friendly faces, a space to work, and refills of jasmine tea.

Inge would like to thank:

My wonderful friends Alex Hartzler, Stephanie Eberle, and Kelley Franceschi for being in my life and supporting me through all my own "impossible choices."

The forest trails of the Bay Area for offering an alternative option to staring at my computer screen.

Lily, my coauthor, for believing in my idea and helping it become a book. I couldn't have done this alone.

Index

Index

Index

Lily Zheng is a diversity, equity, and inclusion consultant who works with organizations around the world to create high-impact and sustainable change. A dedicated change-maker, speaker, and advocate, she writes frequently for publications including the *New York Times*, *Harvard Business Review*, and *HR Executive* and is the coauthor of *Gender Ambiguity in the Workplace: Transgender and Gender-Diverse Discrimination*. She lives in the San Francisco Bay Area with a partner and can frequently be found wearing too much black.

Inge Hansen, PsyD, is a clinical psychologist at Stanford University, where she is the director of student health equity and well-being services. She is also the cofounder and director of the Weiland Health Initiative, which is dedicated to promoting mental health and wellness across all genders and sexualities. She lives in Palo Alto, California, with her son, Judah, who has an abiding passion for Minecraft and frogs.

Berrett–Koehler
Publishers

Berrett-Koehler is an independent publisher dedicated to an ambitious mission: *Connecting people and ideas to create a world that works for all.*

Our publications span many formats, including print, digital, audio, and video. We also offer online resources, training, and gatherings. And we will continue expanding our products and services to advance our mission.

We believe that the solutions to the world's problems will come from all of us, working at all levels: in our society, in our organizations, and in our own lives. Our publications and resources offer pathways to creating a more just, equitable, and sustainable society. They help people make their organizations more humane, democratic, diverse, and effective (and we don't think there's any contradiction there). And they guide people in creating positive change in their own lives and aligning their personal practices with their aspirations for a better world.

And we strive to practice what we preach through what we call "The BK Way." At the core of this approach is *stewardship,* a deep sense of responsibility to administer the company for the benefit of all of our stakeholder groups, including authors, customers, employees, investors, service providers, sales partners, and the communities and environment around us. Everything we do is built around stewardship and our other core values of *quality, partnership, inclusion,* and *sustainability.*

This is why Berrett-Koehler is the first book publishing company to be both a B Corporation (a rigorous certification) and a benefit corporation (a for-profit legal status), which together require us to adhere to the highest standards for corporate, social, and environmental performance. And it is why we have instituted many pioneering practices (which you can learn about at www.bkconnection.com), including the Berrett-Koehler Constitution, the Bill of Rights and Responsibilities for BK Authors, and our unique Author Days.

We are grateful to our readers, authors, and other friends who are supporting our mission. We ask you to share with us examples of how BK publications and resources are making a difference in your lives, organizations, and communities at www.bkconnection.com/impact.

Dear reader,

Thank you for picking up this book and welcome to the worldwide BK community! You're joining a special group of people who have come together to create positive change in their lives, organizations, and communities.

What's BK all about?

Our mission is to connect people and ideas to create a world that works for all.

Why? Our communities, organizations, and lives get bogged down by old paradigms of self-interest, exclusion, hierarchy, and privilege. But we believe that can change. That's why we seek the leading experts on these challenges—and share their actionable ideas with you.

A welcome gift

To help you get started, we'd like to offer you a **free copy** of one of our bestselling ebooks:

www.bkconnection.com/welcome

When you claim your **free ebook**, you'll also be subscribed to our blog.

Our freshest insights

Access the best new tools and ideas for leaders at all levels on our blog at ideas.bkconnection.com.

Sincerely,

Your friends at Berrett-Koehler

Certified

Corporation